Where are the Fighting Giraffes?

College Nickname Edition: A Guide to the Ordinary, Odd, and Outrageous

David Winder

Copyright © 2025 by Feigenwinter Publishing

All rights reserved.

ISBN: 979-8-9912021-5-2

Feigenwinter Publishing
210 Oak Drive S #93
Lake Jackson, TX 77566

feigenwinterpublishing.com

Please email any questions, suggestions, theories, recipes, ramblings, treasure maps, possible schools we may have missed, schools you hope we missed, and of course compliments to wherethegiraffes@gmail.com. This a snapshot of a moment in time – mid-2025. By the time you read this, some of the schools may have adopted new names, been ordered to change nicknames, merged with others, or closed. In conclusion – your school was counted. Probably.

For Saje, Sophia, and Finn who may one day be a Gator, Aggie, Bulldog, Lumberjack, Trojan, Cougar, Bobcat, Tiger, Engineer, Bear, Longhorn, Anteater, Cardinal, Banana Slug, Owl, Wildcat, Sun Devil, Bearkat, Camel, Wolverine, Volunteer, Boll Weevil, Red Raider, Cowboy, Boilermaker, Jayhawk, Jumbo, Eph, or Ichabod.

But unfortunately, not a Fighting Giraffe.

Introduction

Collegiate nicknames are a blend of identity, marketing, and mythology, incorporating elements of anarchy, tradition, pageantry, and the occasional tribal war cry. A volatile combination that can lead to pandemonium, fisticuffs, and an instantly regrettable ankle tattoo imploring those nearby to *Fear the Turtle*.

They are also convenient shorthand for students, alumni, and fans to share their like-mindedness and enforce the notion that we are all in this together, at blood drives, library fundraisers, or basketball games. Nicknames function like passwords at sports bars, quietly announcing, "These are my people. We yell at refs together," and "I didn't wash my lucky sweatshirt, and that is the only reason we are winning today."

Roll Tide!

Nothing bonds people together faster than wearing matching colors and shouting abstract nouns. Nicknames are the reason you can yell "Go **Slugs**!" on a random Saturday afternoon and not be institutionalized. They spare you from having to shout, "Please perform admirably, you players from the University of North Carolina at Chapel Hill!" Most importantly, they provide a socially acceptable way to insult others with your school spirit: "Hey **Tigers**! You suck worse than our team! Please don't hit us! Let's drink some moderately-priced beer together!"

Gig'em Aggies!

But nicknames aren't just for sports. They transform students into something larger than themselves. Alumni, decades removed from their last Scantron-induced panic attack, still roam the earth as **Horned Frogs**, **Cougars**, or **Fighting Camels**, which administrators appreciate during giving campaigns.

For fans who never attended the school, nicknames offer paths (T-shirts, bumper stickers, and personalized license plates) to be recognized as a **Buckeye**, **Volunteer**, or **Trojan** without having to sit through a pesky Intro to Western Literature class.

Hook'em Horns!

In the early 1870s, only professional baseball teams, like the Boston **Red Stockings**, Philadelphia **Athletics**, and New Haven **Elm Citys**, used nicknames. American higher education was a sanctuary for the elite class, where scholarly endeavors in rhetoric and moral philosophy prevailed.

Latin mottos invoking veritas and lux were engraved on every stone not covered in ivy, and professors clad in wool suits smelling of pipe tobacco made no mention of the future branding potential of a **Blue Devil**, **Wolverine**, or **Bear**.

Then in 1875, Harvard had a school-wide vote to determine whether the school's official color should be crimson or magenta. Yes, even 150 years ago, they were a bunch of nerds. **Crimson** won, proving once and for all that they could make bold, decisive choices about slightly different shades of red. Harvard alumni and athletic teams began using it as a nickname soon after. It became official in 1910.

Meanwhile, Yale had a bulldog named 'Handsome Dan' roaming the sidelines at athletic events starting in 1889. Yet it wasn't until 1906 when a sportswriter referred to the team as the **Bulldogs** in a recap of a football game against Princeton that the name stuck.

Since then, a couple of thousand colleges and universities have chosen nicknames – some with deep symbolism, some by student election, some with the help of a sportswriter, and some by turning an insult into something honorable. Several schools have done it multiple times.

In the pages ahead, you'll learn more about collegiate nicknames than you ever thought possible: the esteemed, the clever, the oddly spelled, and the weird.

We'll make our way from A to Z with origin stories and unique monikers, which will have you pondering what administrators could have been thinking when they assumed the **Sagehens** would strike fear into the hearts (or beaks) of their opponents.

As you read on, there are a few things to keep in mind:
- There are more than 2,300 public and private colleges and universities in the U.S. with nicknames, using more than 675 monikers.
- Alternate spellings such as **Red Hawks**, **Redhawks**, and **RedHawks**, are considered three separate entries. Typography is identity!
- A school does not need to participate in a sport to be listed. But many do.
- Some schools use a nickname for the men and add a "Lady" for the women (e.g., **Eagles, Lady Eagles**). Only the **Eagles** would be listed in this scenario.

- All types of institutions are included: colleges, universities, community colleges, junior colleges, and technical institutions. If they have claimed a nickname and possibly printed it on a lanyard, then they are in.

This book is divided into three sections. Note that the graphics are artistic representations – not the official school logos, so there is no need to alert the licensing offices. The first section highlights the most curious sobriquets. The second looks at genres because nickname taxonomy is a legitimate field of study. The third dives into the 50 states and Washington, D.C., and shares some of their interesting nickname and facts.

But alas, once again, there are no **Fighting Giraffes**.

Part I:
Nicknames
Peculiar & Rare

49ers

Golden Years: The Yuba College **49ers** (Linda, CA) take their name from the California Gold Rush, which peaked nearby in 1849 – a time when many fortune seekers flooded the area to go bankrupt in another location. The University of North Carolina (UNC) at Charlotte began as the Charlotte College **Owls**. In 1961, the student body voted to become the **49ers**, not because of their love of prospecting, but rather to honor those who fought to stop the school from closing in 1949. It joined the UNC system and got a name change in 1965.

Sandy: In 2018, Long Beach State (Long Beach, CA) retired the **49er** nickname to distance the school from the suffering of Indigenous peoples during the California Gold Rush. Most of their athletic teams are now known as **The Beach** – a name that evokes sunscreen, surfboards, a delightful fragrance created by Kramer on *Seinfeld*, and less moral ambiguity.

Aardvarks

Word Power: Aardvarks? Aardvarks? Any objections? Great! The Pikes Peak State College **Aardvarks** (Colorado Springs, CO) landed their nickname in the most efficient way possible. Legend has it that the students were too busy job-

hunting to waste time on a nickname, so they opened a dictionary, picked the first animal they saw listed, and went back to polishing their résumés.

Meanwhile, the Aims Community College **Aardvarks** (Greeley, CO) picked the same creature in 1967. No word on how post-graduation job anxiety or alphabetical convenience played a role in the selection.

Anteaters

Drawing Interest: The **Anteaters** became the nickname for the University of California, Irvine in a landslide student vote in 1965. Two water polo players suggested the name after seeing an anteater in the popular comic strip *B.C.* and deciding the Irvine **Anteaters** had a prehistoric charm.

Drinking Interest: What if the Irvine water polo team had been reading the popular *Andy Capp* comic strip instead? Would students and alumni be proudly cheering on the Irvine Gambling Drunks? Would application rates have spiked or plummeted? Ask your favorite bartender for their thoughts. Go Boozers!

Banana Slugs

Bearing Fruit: The banana slug is a bright yellow, slow-gliding gastropod found along the West Coast of the United States, including on the campus of the University of California, Santa Cruz (UCSC). The school's coed teams had embraced the creature since it opened in 1965. But when UCSC joined NCAA Division III for athletics in 1980, it needed an official nickname. The chancellor decided on the **Sea Lions**. Outrage ensued. So did an unyielding commitment to slime! Students continued to campaign for the **Banana Slugs** until they got their way in 1986.

Winner Dinner: Your favorite team is guaranteed a National Championship (in any sport) if you eat five banana slugs in 24 hours. No salt. No grill. Just nature's protein tubes covered in slime. Could you? Would your taste buds allow it to happen? Do you have a championship stomach?

Billikens

Trolling: In the early 1900s, America went bonkers for a strange little creature called the Billiken. This pot-bellied, pointy-eared, tuft-of-hair-having imp was supposed to bring good luck – especially if you were gifted one. The Billiken became a pop culture sensation. Stores stocked their shelves with dolls, charms, postcards, and other goods with the creature's likeness. So how did this mythical scamp become the nickname for Saint Louis University (Missouri) instead of just appearing on your great-grandmother's favorite porcelain lamp?

Well, the school's football coach, John Bender, looked a lot like a Billiken. One story claims a cartoonist doodled the resemblance, posted it on the wall of a local drugstore, and people took notice. Another version says the druggist straight-up told Bender, "Coach, you're a real Billiken," which either meant he was lucky or alarmingly ugly. Regardless, the team became known as Bender's **Billikens**, and the name eventually was adopted by the university.

Boilermakers

Brawny: In 1889, Wabash College (Crawfordsville, IN) suffered a shocking 18-4 loss to Purdue University (West Lafayette, IN) in football. Disbelief turned to accusations with fans surmising that Purdue must have fielded an illegal lineup of log haulers, foundry molders, and other giant non-students working at the local rail yards. When Purdue crushed Wabash 44-0 in 1891, a sportswriter with the Daily Argus headlined his story "Slaughter of the Innocents" with a sub-head reading: *Wabash Snowed Completely Under by the Burly Boiler Makers from Purdue*. The Purdue **Boilermakers** took the field the next football season.

Tall Drink: A **Boilermaker** is the only collegiate nickname that shares its name with a cocktail. Would your support increase or decrease if your favorite school rebranded to the Moscow Mules? What about the Fighting Fuzzy Navels? Or the Flaming Doctor Peppers? Discuss with your favorite waitress and report back.

Boll Weevils

Snug as a Bug: On the town square of Enterprise, Alabama, stands a statue of a woman holding a bowl over her head, and perched atop is a cotton-eating bug the size of a toddler with a résumé in agricultural destruction – the boll weevil. Note: the real insect is smaller than a dime.

The statue was gifted to the city in 1919. The bug part? That was bolted on 30 years later. A plaque was also added that says: *In profound appreciation of the boll weevil and what it has done as the Herald of Prosperity.* Translation: *Thanks for wrecking our cotton farms, you glorious bastards!*

Here's the logic: When boll weevils destroyed the region's cotton crops, one visionary farmer in Coffee County said, "Let's try peanuts." Boom! Goober empire unlocked. By 1919, the region was America's peanut capital. A student vote made the Enterprise State Community College **Boll Weevils** official in 1965.

Other Side: The University of Arkansas at Monticello (UAM) **Boll Weevils** adopted the nickname after a speech by the school's president, in which he compared his students to the persistent little pests, before a game against Magnolia A&M in 1925. The UAM women's athletics teams are called the **Cotton Blossoms**.

Buckeyes

Vision Tree: The buckeye nut comes from the Ohio buckeye tree, which thrives across the Midwest. The nut is dark brown with a tan spot – said to resemble the eye of a deer, or "buck-eye." Early Ohio settlers found it charming. Superstitious people decided it brought good luck. Herbalists found it toxic. The Ohio State **Buckeyes** (Columbus, OH) took the field as early as 1919, though the nickname did not become official until 1950.

Leaf Through: In 1968, **Buckeye** players began receiving helmet stickers of a buckeye leaf for exceptional performances. And since then, casual fans have had to wonder why Ohio State players have what looks like botanical contraband on their head gear.

Cardinal

Colorful: Stanford University (CA) is home to the **Cardinal**. Specifically, Cardinal red, which has been the school's official hue since 1891. From 1930 to 1972, Stanford's teams were known as the **Indians**. And then, for nearly a decade, Stanford athletics went by well, Stanford. No mascot. No nickname. Just vibes and some kickass varsity sweaters. In 1981, the school officially adopted **Cardinal** as its nickname, instantly creating a subset of people who would wonder why a specific redbird is considered so dang important to everybody at Stanford.

Chanticleers

Pecking Order: Back in the early 1960s, Coastal Carolina University (Conway, SC) was known as the **Trojans** and operated as an extension campus of the University of South Carolina (USC). Students began campaigning for a new identity – something that paid homage to USC's **Gamecock** nickname while also setting them apart.

So, naturally, they turned to 14th-century English poet Geoffrey Chaucer for guidance. In *The Canterbury Tales*, Chaucer tells *The Nun's Priest's Tale* – a story about a smooth-talking rooster named

Chanticleer. He's the cock of the walk and has the hens swooning. He's also vain, nearly falling victim to a fox who plays to his ego. The backstory of the Coastal Carolina **Chanticleers** and Chaucer is now explained during every television broadcast.

Book It: Which character from classic literature should a school use for a nickname?
- Ahabs
- Captain Underpants
- Gollums
- Hannibals
- Holdens
- Piggys
- Ramonas
- Tyler Durdens

Claim Jumpers

Big Steal: The Columbia College **Claim Jumpers** (Sonora, CA) pay tribute to the morally flexible entrepreneurs of the California Gold Rush – the ones who had no qualms about thieving property and were probably good at dodging pickaxes.

Columbia sits right in the heart of California's historic Mother Lode, where real-life claim jumpers once roamed, schemed, and stole. Let's face it, **Claim Jumpers** does sound somewhat cooler than Unscrupulous Miners.

Cobbers

Kernel of Truth: Back in the 1890s, Concordia College (Moorhead, MN) students weren't exactly living the city life. Surrounded by farmland, they became an easy punchline for the more urban students of nearby Hope Academy (Moorhead, MN). Those city slickers thought they'd be clever, barging onto campus to make fun of Concordia students during events, hollering "Corncobs! Corncobs!" in mocking tones.

Concordia students eventually embraced the insult, adopting **Corncobs** as a nickname. It remained for nearly 30 years before being trimmed down into the sleeker, sportier **Cobbers**. Because when it comes to nicknames, nothing strikes fear into opponents like sweet corn.

Fear the Ear: Hope Academy closed in 1896.

Crimson Tide

Red Alert: The year is 1907. The University of Alabama (Tuscaloosa) takes the field against Alabama Polytechnic Institute (now Auburn University) in a highly anticipated game. There's tension. There's grit. And there's a lot of mud.

Alabama, then known as the **Thin Red Line** – a not-so-great name for a football team – was the underdog. They played tough, held their ground, and the game ended in a 6–6 tie. Birmingham sportswriter Hugh Roberts watched the waves of mud-covered players surging across the field like some angry congealed tomato soup and dubbed the team the **Crimson Tide**. The nickname did not catch on until Zipp Newman, sports editor for The Birmingham News, started using the Alabama **Crimson Tide** regularly in 1919.

Demon Deacons

Wicked: Wake Forest University (Winston-Salem, NC) has one of the most contradictory nicknames in all of college sports: the **Demon Deacons** – part chaos, part church, all alliteration.

The official story goes: In 1922, a student writer named Mayor Parker coined the term **Demon Deacons** in the Old Gold and Black, the school paper, to describe the "devilish" performance of the team in a win over the Trinity **Blue Devils**, now Duke University. One small problem: Trinity won that game, 3–0, and there is no record of the name in the story. The first actual documented use of "Demon Deacons" in print appears to be from 1923, but it doesn't explain why they chose that term. So what gives Wake Forest?

Questionable: Still more questions than answers …
- Would the **Diamond Deacons** be a more marketable name?
- Did the writer's future self go back in time with a DeLorean time machine, take his college self to a future win over Trinity, and cause several humorous misunderstandings, including the nickname issue?
- Does a **Demon Deacon** preach with malice?

Dirtbags

Filthy: Long Beach State (CA) baseball was rebuilding – figuratively and literally in 1989. The team didn't have its own field. Instead, they practiced at a local park that was just dirt with some optimism. No grass. No glam.

An assistant coach jokingly referred to it as "Dirtbag Field." The players loved it. The name stuck – first as a badge of survival, then as a full-on identity. Players were soon earning Dirtbags T-shirts for their hustle and toughness. It worked as the team made it to the College World Series.

Music Theory: There is no truth to the rumor that a week at Long Beach baseball camp led the band Wheatus to write the hit song *Teenage Dirtbag*.

Ducks

Fit the Bill: The University of Oregon (Eugene, OR) was initially known as the **Webfoots**. That nickname originated from a group of Massachusetts fishermen, known as the Webfoots, who fought in the Revolutionary War. After the war, "Webfoot" became a broader nickname for New Englanders. When many of them later moved to Oregon, they brought the name with them.

In the early 1900s, Oregon students referred to themselves as **Webfoots**. The sports editor of *The Oregonian* started working the name into his stories. But eventually, headline writers, tired of having **Webfoots** take up so much space, began referring to the teams as the **Ducks** instead. The students liked the change and voted for **Ducks** in two nickname elections, beating Timberwolves, Lumberjacks, Trappers, and Pioneers.

Flock Together: The Stevens Institute of Technology (Hoboken, NJ) is also the **Ducks**. The mascot is Attila the Duck.

Ephs

Naming Names: The Williams College **Ephs** (Williamstown, MA) is a tribute to Colonel Ephraim Williams, a colonial soldier who died in 1755 at the Battle of Lake George during the French and Indian War. He left a will that provided money for the creation of a free school in West Township, on the condition that the town be renamed Williamstown.

Bequeathing: Any reader who adjusts their will to require their town to be renamed Fighting Giraffe City to receive funds will be automatically entered into a drawing for a free book. (Town must be officially renamed. Reader must be dead. Fighting Giraffeville also eligible.)

Eutectics

All Systems Go: The University of Health Sciences and Pharmacy (St. Louis, MO) was initially known as the **Volunteers**. However, in 1993, the school rebranded itself into something a bit more scientific – the **Eutectics**! A eutectic system refers to the process where two solids combine to form a liquid at a lower melting point than either of the individual components. If that name doesn't fire you up to go out and knock somebody's head off, you might be dead inside. Check with your family doctor.

Fighting Artichokes

Battle Plants: The Scottsdale Community College (SCC) **Fighting Artichokes** (AZ) is a nickname born of sarcasm. In 1972, SCC was facing a funding dilemma, and students were protesting budget priorities favoring athletics over academics. Amid the unrest, an election was held to change the SCC nickname, which was then the **Drovers**. Students voted to embarrass the administration by stuffing the ballot box with the most ridiculous nickname they could devise.

Go **Artichokes**!

Leaders called for a do-over election, and the **Artichokes** won again. Students eventually began to rally behind the absurd nickname. Someone added a hostile modifier later for those who dared to disrespect vegetables.

Quarrelsome Food: The official nickname for Delta State (Cleveland, MS) is the **Statesmen**, but few recognize them by that name. They are known as the **Fighting Okra** – an alternative nickname coined by students in the late 1980s. The University of North Carolina School of the Arts **Fighting Pickles** (Winston-Salem, NC) was named after the school held a contest for a nickname in 1972. The name was submitted by a group of students in honor of an oboe player they knew who was always searching for the perfect pickle.

Fighting Giraffes, Where Art Thou?

By a Neck: The world of collegiate nicknames includes the Yakima Valley **Yaks** (Yakima, WA), Cuyahoga Community **Triceratops** (Cuyahoga County, OH), and the Sweet Briar **Vixens** (Sweet Briar, VA), but there are no **Fighting Giraffes** to be found.

Tall, graceful, surprisingly aggressive when provoked. What more could a school want in a nickname?

Fighting Illini

Clashing: The University of Illinois **Fighting Illini** (Champaign-Urbana, IL) nickname traces back to the Illiniwek confederation, a group of 12 or 13 Native American tribes that once lived in the Mississippi River Valley. It is also where the state of Illinois gets its name from. The Illini people were relocated in the 18th century to what are now the states of Kansas and Oklahoma.

In 1874, the Illinois student newspaper changed its name to *The Illini*, which soon became a catch-all term for the university's students, staff, and athletic teams.

Fighting Irish

Attacking: There are multiple theories about why the University of Notre Dame (South Bend, IN) is known as the **Fighting Irish**. The school's original nickname was the **Catholics**, then later the **Ramblers**.

Some stories trace the name back to Irish soldiers who fought in the Civil War. Others point to a Notre Dame player demanding his Irish teammates play better against Michigan in 1909 because they were not fighting worth a lick.

Most likely, the **Fighting Irish** began as an anti-Catholic and anti-Irish insult, and Notre Dame flipped it into a badge of honor. The nickname became official in 1927.

Gamecocks

Crowing: The South Carolina College **Jaguars**, now known as the University of South Carolina, pulled off a big upset by beating the rival Clemson **Tigers** 12-6 in 1902 at the state fair. To celebrate, students unveiled a poster of a gamecock standing victorious over a beaten tiger – a peak 1900s Palmetto State cockfighting taunt.

Clemson students warned their rivals not to bring the artwork to the parade the next day. Naturally, the South Carolina students showed up with their poultry propaganda. Enraged Clemson cadets brought sabers. South Carolina students responded with pistols, knives, and other weapons.

It was like the Sharks vs. the Jets, without the dancing and singing. Police and professors intervened to convince the students to burn the drawing, so that everyone could calm down.

In the aftermath, the game was canceled for six years. But South Carolina took the field in 1903 as the **Gamecocks**. The name honors both a Revolutionary War hero – South Carolina militia general Thomas Sumter, known as "The Fighting Gamecock" – and the school's legendary ability to escalate a football win into a street brawl due to artwork.

Belligerent Birds: The Jacksonville State University **Gamecocks** (Jacksonville, AL) switched from the **Eagle Owls** because students wanted a tougher nickname.

The Delaware **Blue Hens** (Newark, DE) honor a Revolutionary War company called the Delaware Regiment. Captain John Caldwell was fond of cockfighting and brought his favorite fighting chickens from his farm. The company became known as the Blue Hens' Chickens.

Geoducks

Mussel Beach: The Evergreen State College **Geoducks** (Olympia, WA) are named after the world's largest burrowing clam (weighing more than two pounds and living three feet below the surface).

These bivalve mollusks, pronounced "gooey ducks," can live for more than 100 years in the salt water of the Pacific Northwest. Evergreen State chose them as their nickname because they represent those who are willing to dig deep to succeed.

Gorillas

Monkeying Around: The Pittsburg State **Gorillas** (Pittsburg, KS) started as a pep club, created in 1923 to foster school spirit, enthusiasm, and supervise freshman hazing.

At the time, a gorilla represented roughnecks or untamed rowdiness, which was perfect for a club that claimed to want pep at all times. In 1925, the school adopted **Gorillas** as its official nickname.

In 1989, the women's athletics team voted to change from the **Gussies**, named after a major supporter, to the **Gorillas**.

War of Words: What other 1920s slang would you want as a new nickname for your school? Write your coach today!

- Brunos
- Can Openers
- Goombahs
- Goons
- Hoodlums
- Hooligans
- Jobbies
- Lugs
- Palookas
- Plug-Uglies
- Punks
- Saps
- Thugs
- Tramps
- Yeggs

Hatters

Heads Up: The Stetson University **Hatters** (DeLand, FL) is what happens when a hat manufacturer becomes involved in higher education. In 1886, a brutal freeze decimated Florida's citrus industry and with it, the finances of Henry DeLand, founder of DeLand Academy.

Faced with financial collapse, DeLand turned to a friend who didn't grow oranges but did happen to run a hat empire: John B. Stetson, creator of the iconic Stetson hat, who stepped in with a donation for the school.

In 1889, DeLand requested that Stetson be made Chairman of the Board and the school be renamed Stetson University. In 1901, the school fielded its first football team, nicknamed the **Hatters** in honor of Stetson.

Hawkeyes

Lost Definition: The Iowa **Hawkeyes** (Iowa City, IA) take their nickname from Iowa's official moniker as the Hawkeye State, which sounds cool, but no one knows what it is. There is no record of its meaning or why it became the state's nickname. The first recorded mention dates to 1859. Some believe the name is derived from a character in *The Last of the Mohicans* by James Fenimore Cooper, which debuted in 1826.

Hokies

Cheerful: If you've ever watched a Virginia Tech (Blacksburg, VA) football game and thought, "What in the heck is a Hokie?" You're not alone. Even some Virginians are unsure.

In 1896, the school held a contest for a new cheer to boost school spirit. A student won $5 for writing a cheer that started with the phrase: "Hoki, Hoki, Hoki, Hy." The words mean nothing. He just thought they sounded exciting. To make pronunciation easier, an "e" was added. The term "Hokie" eventually became associated with the school's students, athletes, and fans. As in: "Yeah, I'm a Hokie. Please don't ask me what that means."

But before the **Hokies** could stick, the **Gobblers** became more popular. There are many stories about how that came to be, but the most prevalent is that athletes would scarf down meals at such impressive speeds that people said they "gobbled up" their food. Soon after, a trained turkey that could do tricks started showing up at the games.

Fast forward to the early 1980s, head football Coach Bill Dooley heard the origin of the nickname and wasn't thrilled that his football program was associated with cafeteria speed-eating. He then led the charge to reclaim the nickname as the **Hokies**.

Bird Watcher: The turkey didn't go quietly, though. Virginia Tech's mascot evolved into the HokieBird — a leaner, cooler, more muscular version of the Gobbler.

Hoosiers

Who Can Say: Indiana University (Bloomington, IN) has proudly been the **Hoosiers** for more than a century. It was an easy name to pick since Indiana is the Hoosier state.

However, no one can say with absolute certainty where the word "Hoosier" originated or what it means – it's mysterious, disputed, and debated. Historians and residents have many theories, including frontiersmen questioning visitors, "Who's here?" But none have been proven.

Horned Frogs

Bloody Reptiles: When you see the Texas Christian University **Horned Frogs** (Fort Worth, TX) on TV, remember this: They are named after a lizard.

Back in 1897, when TCU was still called AddRan Christian University, students were putting together a yearbook and realized they needed a name for it. Luckily, the football field was crawling

with Texas horned lizards – round- bodied, spiky little beasts that look like frogs and have a weird talent: They can shoot blood from their eyes up to five feet. Naturally, the students were like, "That's our spirit animal, but marketing matters. Let's call them **Horned Frogs** instead of Spiny Blood Lizards!"

Ichabods

Crowning Glory: The Washburn University **Ichabods** (Topeka, KS) derives its school name and nickname from Ichabod Washburn, a prominent financial supporter. Students started referring to themselves as **Ichabods** in the late 1800s, and then injured (we guess) anyone who attempted to change it.

Old Timer: Which late 1800s first name do you wish your favorite school had picked for a nickname?
- Asahels
- Dorcas
- Ebenezers
- Eliphalets
- Gertrudes
- Peregrines
- Rufuses
- Zebulons
- Zilphas

Jayhawks

Fight or Flight: The University of Kansas **Jayhawks** (Lawrence, KS) nickname is not a bird. The term can be traced back to the 1840s, when the Kansas Territory was filled with anti-slavery and pro-slavery settlers, both of whom identified as Jayhawks or Jayhawkers. Over time, the free staters (the anti-slavery faction) became known as the Jayhawkers, and during the Civil War, a regiment known as the Mounted Kansas Jayhawks was formed. Eventually, the name came to represent the people of Kansas, which is where the university gets its nickname.

Jumbos

Elephant in the Room: The Tufts University **Jumbos** (Medford, MA) is the only college in America named after an actual elephant. Not a metaphor. Not a statue. A gigantic, world-famous elephant named Jumbo.

In the 1880s, P.T. Barnum, the great ringmaster behind the Barnum & Bailey Circus, was a major benefactor of Tufts. So when Jumbo tragically died in a train accident in 1885, Barnum had him stuffed and donated the remains to Tufts. The massive Jumbo was installed in the university's Barnum Hall.

He became a kind of unofficial mascot – students would place pennies on his trunk for good luck before exams or dates (probably). By the early 1900s, Tufts athletic teams were being called the **Jumbos**.

Barnum Hall burned down in 1975, and Jumbo was believed to have been lost in the fire. But not entirely. A secretary saved some of his ashes, and today they're kept in a peanut butter jar in the athletic director's office. A 5,000-pound bronze statue of Jumbo was added to the campus in 2015.

Keelhaulers

Sea of Hurt: The Cal Poly Maritime **Keelhaulers** (Vallejo, CA) nickname honors corporal punishment on the high seas. The Dutch and English navies, and some pirates, disciplined sailors for egregious conduct by tying their hands to a rope and hauling them from one side of the ship to the other under the keel (the bottom-most part of the ship). The practice was outlawed in 1853. A school vote made **Keelhaulers** the official nickname in 1974 because how often do you get an opportunity to immortalize nautical torture?

Lady Techsters

Doggone It: When Sonja Hogg took over the women's basketball program at Louisiana Tech University (Ruston, LA) in the 1970s, she vetoed the Lady Bulldogs nickname – a feminine version of the school's mascot. Her reason? "I could just hear people saying, 'There comes Coach Hogg and all her little bitches.'"

Instead, she came up with **Lady Techsters** as a nickname. In 2023, Louisiana Tech decided that all sports except women's basketball would be called the **Bulldogs**. The **Lady Techsters** would remain.

Little Giants

Big Trouble: The Wabash College **Little Giants** (Crawfordsville, IN) received their nickname from an Indianapolis sportswriter in 1904. He was impressed by the football team's performance against larger schools with much bigger players. It is unknown if they ran a trick play called the Annexation of Puerto Rico. (See the 1994 movie *Little Giants* if you're confused)

Longhorns

Cattle Guard: In 1903, the University of Texas did not have a nickname. Alex Weisberg, the editor-in-chief of the school newspaper, found that unacceptable. He ordered his sports reporter to call the school's teams the **Longhorns**, the popular breed of beef cattle with the long horns, at every opportunity. A newspaper in Oklahoma City referred to the football team as the Texas Rangers, but that did not catch on. By 1907, all the Texas teams were using the **Longhorns** nickname.

Lyons

Twin Sisters: The nickname **Lyons** is used by two schools as a tribute to Mary Lyon, a champion for women's education in 19th-century America. In 1834, Lyon worked as a visiting instructor and curriculum consultant for the Wheaton Female Seminary (now Wheaton College in Norton, MA). A few years later, she founded the Mount Holyoke Female Seminary (now Mount Holyoke College in South Hadley, MA).

Craft Time: Congratulations! Your last name is becoming a collegiate nickname. First, do you want to add an adjective, such as 'Defiant' or 'Middling', for some extra flavor? Will the name be plural? Next, ask AI to create a logo based on the new nickname and your occupation. Now, hit up the local tattoo parlor. Please inform the artist that you would like this design to be tattooed on your shoulder. Promise not to cry. **Warning**: By purchasing this book, you're officially committed to a tattoo. If you stole this book, then you must get two tattoos. Please send us photos like this soon-to-be tattoo.

Mean Green

Discourteous: The University of North Texas (Denton, TX) is known as the **Mean Green** because a fan begged the then **Eagles** to play better by getting angry. In 1966, Sidney Sue Graham used then-North Texas State University's school colors to make her point vociferously: "Come on, green! Get mean!" and "Here we go, mean green."

She quite liked her "Mean Green" cheers and told her husband, who was the school's sports information director. He later included the term in a press release, and the name slowly caught on, becoming the football team's moniker in 1968. In 2000, UNT officially adopted the **Mean Green** nickname for all teams.

Angry: UNT legend Joe Greene didn't become "Mean Joe Greene" until he was drafted by the Pittsburgh Steelers in 1968, and the local media gave him the nickname. Then he traded a Coke for a jersey and the rest is history.

Nittany Lions

On the Mountain: Back in 1904, Penn State's (State College, PA) Harrison Mason heard an opposing player bragging about the toughness of the Princeton **Tigers**. Not to be outdone, Mason hyped up the Nittany Lion – a mountain lion that prowled on Mount Nittany, located near the Penn State campus. He didn't stop at bragging; he launched a PR campaign, starting a humor magazine under a fake name just to promote the nickname to students and administrators. By 1907, the **Nittany Lions** was officially Penn State's nickname.

Penguins

Ice Cold: The Youngstown State **Penguins** (Youngstown, OH) nickname is a result of a cold night in West Virginia against West Liberty State Teachers College. The most popular theory involves an unheated bus ride to the game and a freezing visitors' locker room. When the players finally made it to the court, they were frozen stiff, so they moved their arms and legs like penguins as they tried to get warm, which caught the eye of some students in attendance. By the time they returned to campus, using **Penguins** as a nickname was already catching on. It became official in December 1933.

Habitual: The Dominican University of California (San Rafael, CA) is also known as the **Penguins**. Students voted to change the nickname from **Hounds** in the early 1970s to honor the Dominican Sisters, who wore their distinctive long black-and-white habits.

Rainbow Warriors

True Colors: The University of Hawaii (Honolulu, HI) was known as the **Deans** up until the last game of the 1923 season, when they upset the Oregon State **Beavers** 7-0 while a rainbow appeared over the field. From then on, they were the **Rainbows**, eventually becoming the **Rainbow Warriors** in the early 1970s. The women's athletics program was given the **Rainbow Wahine** nickname in 1972 – wahine means "women" in Hawaiian.

Razorbacks

Hog Wild: In 1895, students at the University of Arkansas had a vote to determine the official school color: Cardinal red or heliotrope – that's purple with a hint of pink. Thankfully for area merchandisers, red won, so the school became the **Cardinals**.

The name lost its popularity after a little over a decade, with students and sportswriters suggesting other nicknames. Football Coach Hugo Bezdek galvanized them in 1909 by describing his team as "playing like a wild band of razorbacks," after a 16-0 win over LSU. By the following year, the **Razorbacks** were official.

Around the Horn: If heliotrope had won, would they have been the Unicorns?

Rougarous

Ah-Hoo! Werewolves of Louisiana: The River Parishes Community College **Rougarous** (Gonzales, LA) nickname is straight out of Cajun folklore. According to legend, the rougarou is a swamp-dwelling beast with the body of a human and the head of a wolf that hunts down misbehaving children, lapsed Catholics, and anyone else who hasn't been living right. Trying to escape a werewolf while also nursing a hangover does not sound fun.

Believers can protect themselves by keeping 13 items at their door. The monster's tragic weakness is that it can't count above 12. It'll spend all night getting confused before giving up at sunrise. Raise your hand if you know that feeling!

Monster Mash: What homegrown cryptid should your local college use as inspiration for a nickname?
- A shapeshifter who haunts students who haven't filled out their FAFSA applications
- A Wi-Fi demon that interrupts presentations, forcing students to start over continuously
- A cursed golem who resets students' passwords and usernames to match their worst fears

Sasquatch

Legendary: In the misty forests of the Pacific Northwest, few creatures are more iconic than **Bigfoot** – except maybe his doppelgänger, **Sasquatch**. So when the Community Colleges of Spokane (WA) decided to rebrand, they didn't abandon the legendary wood ape – they just gave it a glow-up.

Market research revealed that the **Bigfoot** logo – an actual big foot – was not popular. So they changed **Bigfoot's** big foot logo, which also could be a Sasquatch foot, to the face of a menacing **Sasquatch**, which could also be a menacing **Bigfoot**. In the process, they changed from one forest legend to another. Same blurry forest dweller. Sassy new attitude.

Sea Beggars

Shiver Me Timbers: The Providence Christian College **Sea Beggars** (Pasadena, CA) dug deep into Reformation history for their nickname – like, 16th-century Dutch-Calvinist-pirate deep. During the Eighty Years' War, Dutch privateers called the Watergeuzen helped fight off the massive Spanish Armada and secure Dutch independence. Sure, Watergeuzen sounds like a terrible collegiate nickname, but in English, it translates to Sea Beggars, which sounds much more confusing. Providence Christian chose the name to honor its Dutch Calvinist heritage and, presumably, its students' shared commitment to sailing through finals without sinking.

Sooners

Trading Places: The University of Oklahoma **Sooners** (Norman, OK) nickname proudly honors those who break the rules. During the Oklahoma Land Run of the late 1800s, settlers raced to claim chunks of land, but some folks decided to sneak in before the starting pistol sounded. Those land-grabbers were dubbed Sooners, as in "they got there sooner than they should have." The term was basically frontier slang for "cheater," but over time it got a makeover into "ambitious go-getter."

Sound

Pump Up the Volume: When your campus includes the John Lennon Center for Music and Technology, you're not going to be the Eels or Woodchucks. Five Towns College (Dix Hills, NY), which offers majors including music performance and audio production, embraced its internal music nerd and went with the **Sound**. Hopefully, they also considered Feedback, Reverbs, and Fightin' Cow Bells.

Stormy Petrels

Drop in the Ocean: The Oglethorpe University **Stormy Petrels** (Brookhaven, GA) nickname honors the founder of the Georgia colony and the school's namesake, James Oglethorpe. According to legend, Oglethorpe was crossing the Atlantic Ocean in 1732 and was inspired by the courage and perseverance of the small seabirds he saw, diving into the crashing waves to find food. It is said that the school's motto, Nescit Cedere, which means "Small. Scrappy. Perpetually soggy." is based on the Stormy Petrel. Wait! Bad translation. It means, "He does not know how to give up."

Student Princes

Royal Treatment: In 1926, a Heidelberg University (Tiffin, OH) press agent walked past a theater billboard advertising the Broadway operetta *The Student Prince*, a hit show about a young German prince attending the University of Heidelberg (Germany). In the story, the prince is shipped off to university, where he hates everything, but then he drinks a bunch of beer, makes some poor decisions, bonds with some cool friends, sings his heart out, and falls in love with a barmaid. So, just like every other liberal arts semester abroad.

The press agent liked the title, saw the name connection, and decided to have a little fun. In the very next issue of *The Heidelberg Bulletin*, he referred to the football team as the **Student Princes**. Soon after, it was the official nickname.

Tar Heels

Sticky Situation: The University of North Carolina **Tar Heels** (Chapel Hill, NC) nickname dates back to the 1800s, when the state was the leading producer of goods for the naval industry, including tar, pitch, and turpentine. It was a sticky business, and sometimes the workers would go barefoot in the summer and end up with tar on their feet.

The term "Tar Heel" became an insult for laborers doing the dirty work. During the Civil War, North Carolina soldiers embraced the nickname and became renowned for their toughness and refusal to retreat. Soon, the term became an expression of state pride, including the University of North Carolina adopting the nickname in the 1880s.

Tars

Paint It Black: The Rollins College **Tars** (Winter Park, FL) nickname refers to 18th-century sailors, known as "jack tars," who were often covered in tar from patching sails, waterproofing ships, and generally doing all the things that make pirate cosplay seem wildly inaccurate.

Valiants

Crown Princes: Manhattanville University (Purchase, NY) owes its nickname to a father who refused to let boredom win. In 1974, while watching his son's team get thumped by Sarah Lawrence University, Tim Cohane Sr. drifted into a medieval daydream, as one does, and thought of Prince Valiant from the comics. He remembered a quote from French courtier Jacques Coeur: "To the valiant of heart, nothing is impossible."

That's all the inspiration he needed. Manhattanville mounted a comeback, and he proposed his nickname, **Valiants**, which stuck. The women's teams, previously known as the **Villains**, changed their name to **Valiants** in 1978. Moral of the story: Never underestimate a dad, a blowout game, and a wandering mind full of knights.

Volunteers

Helping Hands: When the U.S. government needed help during the War of 1812, Tennessee basically said, "Hold my moonshine." More than 1,500 men, led by future President Andrew Jackson, volunteered and helped win the Battle of New Orleans. Then in 1835, a bunch of Tennesseans, including the ever-quotable Davy Crockett, went to fight for Texas independence.

When the government asked for 2,600 troops for the Mexican-American War in 1846, Tennessee sent 30,000. The Volunteer State was born, and the University of Tennessee (Knoxville, TN) proudly adopted the **Volunteers** nickname.

Wasps

Swarm Over: The Emory & Henry University **Whitetoppers** (Emory, VA) were holding their own, only trailing 6-0 at halftime against the heavily favored Tennessee **Volunteers** in 1921.

Sportswriters were so impressed with the **Whitetoppers**' stingy defense that they began to refer to the players as wasps because of the way they swarmed the ball.

The game ended in a 27-0 loss, but not long after, the **Wasps** became the school's official nickname. The following season, Tennessee rolled out its fumigation formation and cruised to a 50-0 victory over the pests.

Mountain Do: The **Whitetoppers** nickname was used 1920-21 and refers to nearby Whitetop Mountain.

Wonder Boys

Astonishing: The Second District Agricultural School **Aggies** (Russellville, AR), now Arkansas Tech, had a big game in 1920 against the Henderson-Brown College **Reddies** – now Henderson State University. After a scoreless first half, the **Aggies** made some plays in the second half to win 13-0.

The Arkansas Gazette had been impressed with the Russellville team's play, especially standout John Tucker, during the year, referring to them as a "wonder team" multiple times.

After beating the **Reddies**, the headline the next day celebrated the **Wonder Boys**. The name caught on with students and alums and became official soon after.

The Arkansas Tech women's teams were known as the **Wonder Girls** or **Wonderettes** until 1975, when a vote decided they would be called the **Golden Suns**.

Zips

Getting the Boot: In 1925, the University of Akron (OH) asked its students to choose the school's nickname from a collection of nominations so strange that they may have been a psychological experiment gone wrong.

The choices included Rubbernecks, Hillbillies, Zippers, Tip Toppers, Cheveliers, and the Golden Blue Devils (when one color just won't do).

The winner was the **Zippers**, the name taken from the rubber galoshes with metal fasteners created by the local B.F. Goodrich Company. The school shortened the name to the **Zips** in 1952 to avoid confusion with the garment industry.

Part II: Popular Genres & Nicknames

Adjectives

Categorize: More than 250 schools felt the need to add descriptors to give their nicknames some extra pizzazz or additional oomph, including those that are:

- Fearsome: Immaculata **Mighty Macs** (Chester County, PA)
- Gritty: South Carolina – Beaufort **Sand Sharks** (Beaufort, SC)
- Heavenly: Meredith College **Avenging Angels** (Raleigh, NC)
- Metropolitan: Academy of Art University **Urban Knights** (San Francisco, CA)
- Socks: Presbyterian College **Blue Hose** (Clinton, SC)
- Stings: St. Ambrose **Fighting Bees** (Davenport, IA)

Dream Matchup: **Avenging Angels** vs. **Urban Knights**. Coming this fall, a no-holds-barred, art-school-meets-apocalypse thriller where divine vengeance battles metro armor to see who will

rule the university's streets in *Midterm Mayhem: Halo vs. Helmet*. The winner gets the **Fighting Bees** in the sequel.

Aggies

Cream of the Crop: The Morrill Land-Grant Acts of 1862 and 1890 established universities aiming to educate students for a growing industrial society in subjects like agronomy, animal science, military tactics, and engineering.

Many of those schools leaned into their agricultural identity, with nicknames such as **Aggies** or **Farmers**. Today, 10 schools still hold onto the **Aggies** nickname, including those that are:
- Ginormous: Texas A&M (College Station, TX)
- Historically Black: North Carolina A&T State (Greensboro, NC)
- Neighborly: New Mexico State (Las Cruces, NM); Doña Ana CC (Las Cruces, NM)
- Oklahoman: Cameron University (Lawton, OK); Oklahoma Panhandle State (Goodwell)
- Public Ivy: University of California, Davis
- Record Holder for Kissing Couples: Utah State (Logan, UT)
- Roots in Jewish Agrarianism: Delaware Valley University (Doylestown, PA)
- Small: Nebraska College of Technical Agriculture (Curtis, NE)

Change Over: As schools evolved into more comprehensive research universities, many chose to move away from their agrarian roots and select other nicknames, and in some cases, change the school's name altogether. Schools that were once known as **Aggies** include Arkansas State, Colorado State, Connecticut, Kansas State, Massachusetts, Michigan State, Mississippi State, North Carolina State, Oklahoma State, Oregon State, and Rhode Island.

Agriculture

Bet the Farm: Many schools have moved on from their farm-fresh origins and given up the pitchfork for something flashier. However, even with the rebrand, agriculture remains deeply ingrained in higher education.

More than 70 colleges and universities still carry the soil-stained spirit of their agrarian roots. Beyond the classic **Aggies** or **Cowboys**, you'll find those with nicknames with some rural ties, including those that are:

- Cultivators: Dallas Eastfield **Harvesters** (Mesquite, TX)
- Grainy: Wichita State **Shockers** (Wichita, KS)
- Loud: West Virginia Northern **Thundering Chickens** (Wheeling, WV)
- Stalkers (non-weird): Nebraska **Cornhuskers** (Lincoln, NE)
- Stone Cold: Bethel **Threshers** (North Newton, KS)
- Who You're Gonna Call: Garden City **Broncbusters** (Garden City, KS)

Hunger After: Which restaurant would you rather eat at, **Shockers** or **Thundering Chickens**?

Alternative Spellings

Road Less Taken: Give me a K! Trust us, we know it sounds odd, but that's how we spell it! No need to pontificate further! There are more than 15 sets of collegiate nicknames that feature at least one alternate spelling, including those that are:
- Binturongs: Sam Houston State **Bearkats** (Huntsville, TX)
- French: Dillard **Bleu Devils** (New Orleans, LA)
- Mythical: Missouri Western State **Griffons** (Saint Joseph, MO); Sarah Lawrence **Gryphons** (Yonkers, NY); **Griffins** (9)
- Not Indoors: Allegheny County **Wild Cats** (Alleghany, PA)
- Tempestuous: Rio Grande **RedStorm** (Rio Grande, OH)
- Wild: Central Oklahoma **Bronchos** (Edmond, OK)
- Winging It: Indiana University – Northwest **RedHawks** (Gary, IN)

Dream Matchup: **RedHawks** vs. **RedStorm**. The loser has to add a space.

Amphibians

Cold Blooded: Only two schools have taken the amphibian route for their nicknames – the North Seattle **Tree Frogs** (Seattle, WA) and the Quinebaug Valley CC **Frogs** (Danielson, CT). Which unused amphibian would be a great collegiate nickname?
- Axolotls
- Blue Poison Dart Frogs
- Giant Salamanders
- Godzillas

Animals

Feature Creatures: From fuzzy to ferocious, if it walks, flies, slithers, or stings, there's a decent chance it's already representing someone's alma mater on a hoodie. Members of Kingdom Animalia range from the tiny (**Bees**) to the gigantic (**Polar Bears**) to the venomous (**Cobras**) to the jumpy (**Kangaroos**) and combine to make up more than 50% of all collegiate nicknames.

All told, there are more than 1,250 schools representing a bunch of different critters (real and imagined) that are:
- Aggressive: Mary Baldwin **Fighting Squirrels** (Staunton, VA)
- Alliterate: Yakima Valley **Yaks** (Yakima, WA)
- Bright: Fresno Pacific **Sunbirds** (Fresno, CA)
- Diggers: Wisconsin-Green Bay at Sheboygan **Wombats** (Sheboygan, WI)
- Jumpy: South Dakota State **Jackrabbits** (Brookings, SD)
- Mouthy: Spoon River **Snappers** (Canton, IL)
- Painful: South Carolina-Sumter **Fire Ants** (Sumter, SC)
- Singers: Alaska Southeast **Humpback Whales** (Juneau, AK)
- Stepping On It: Oregon Institute of Technology **Hustlin' Owls** (Klamath Falls, OR)
- Valuable: Minnesota **Golden Gophers** (Minneapolis, MN)

Face the Music: Which band are you going to see? The Fire Ants, The Hustlin' Owls, or The Humpback Snappers? Consult your favorite bass player for more information.

Bearcats

Compound Word: Of the 11 schools that proudly call themselves the **Bearcats** (or the Sam Houston State **Bearkats**), exactly zero have ever spotted a real bearcat (aka the binturong) lumbering across campus.

So why the name? Most schools probably thought they were going with some adorable teddy bear that purrs.

The Cincinnati **Bearcats** (Cincinnati, OH) nickname dates to 1914 when star football player Leonard "Teddy" Baehr was the talk of the campus.

A chant was created during a game against Kentucky that went, "They may be **Wildcats**, but we have Baehr-cat on our side." Soon after, a cartoon featuring the "Cincinnati Bear Cats" appeared in the school paper.

Birds

Feathered Friends: There are more than 1,000 species of birds found in the U.S., but only a relative few have become collegiate nicknames. The **Cardinals**, **Eagles**, **Falcons**, **Hawks**, and **Owls** make up the majority, but in total, there are more than 375 schools with bird nicknames, including those that are:

- Flying Colors: Century College **Wood Ducks** (White Bear Lake, MN)
- Frosty: Lake Superior **IceHawks** (Duluth, MN)
- Long Tailed: Miami Hamilton **Harriers** (Hamilton, OH)
- Majestic: Oxnard **Condors** (Oxnard, CA)
- Pugilistic: College of the Mainland **Fighting Ducks** (Texas City, TX)
- Salty: Salisbury University **Sea Gulls** (Salisbury, MD)
- Scorching: Tennessee Southern **Firehawks** (Pulaski, TN)

Dream Matchup: **Firehawks** vs. **IceHawks**. The age-old question in Hawk form.

Blue Devils

Diabolical: There are 10 schools with the nickname **Blue Devils**, including the most well-known Duke University (Durham, NC). Duke's **Blue Devil** nickname can be traced back to World War I, when renowned French soldiers – the Chasseurs Alpins, also known as les Diables Bleus – made the name famous worldwide with their fighting in the Alps. When Duke started searching for a new nickname in 1920, fans of the legendary soldiers nominated it, but no decision was made. In 1922, the editors of the school's publications started calling the athletic teams the **Blue Devils**, steadily gaining acceptance.

Bruins

Bear Down: The **Bruins** is the nickname for eight schools, the largest being the University of California, Los Angeles (UCLA). Founded as the southern branch of the University of California in 1919, UCLA's first official nickname was the **Cubs**, keeping it in the family with the northern branch – California, Berkeley **Golden Bears**. Soon, UCLA decided it wanted to be fully grown, changing its nickname to the **Grizzlies**. In 1926, it applied to join the Pacific Coast Conference, which already had the University of Montana **Grizzlies**. Montana refused to share the nickname, so UCLA went to work thinking of replacement bear names – Kodiaks, Silvertips, and Bruins were among the considered options. Cal Berkeley, who was using **Bruins** as an alternative nickname, acquiesced after some heated debates and gave the name to UCLA in 1926.

Bulldogs

Bark Days: The **Bulldogs** are the fourth most popular collegiate nickname, with more than 50 schools.

- Yale University (New Haven, CT) had a bulldog named Handsome Dan, which patrolled the football sidelines, giving rise to its nickname.
- The University of Georgia (Athens, GA) athletics website says the school may have borrowed the nickname from Yale, along with its president and blueprints to some buildings.
- The Butler University (Indianapolis, IN) student newspaper was trying to think of a new nickname for the school when a bulldog meandered into the office, giving the students an idea. Legend has it that the dog was looking for work, but its résumé was a little ruff.

Christian

Faithful: The most popular nicknames for Christian-affiliated schools are the **Eagles, Tigers,** and **Warriors**. All told, there are more than 650 Christian-affiliated colleges and universities with nicknames, including those that are:
- Aggressive Clergy: North Carolina Wesleyan **Battling Bishops** (Rocky Mount, NC)
- Also, Aggressive Clergy: Ohio Wesleyan **Battling Bishops** (Delaware, OH)
- Ecclesiastic: Snead State **Parsons** (Boaz, AL)
- Gallant: Evangel University **Valor** (Springfield, MO)
- Homage: Anna Maria College **AmCats** (Pulaski, TN)
- Noble: Crown College **Royal Crusaders** (Powell, TN)
- Truculent Paragons: Carroll College **Fighting Saints** (Helena, MT)
- Truculent Paragons, Too: St. Francis **Fighting Saints** (Joliet, IL)

Dream Matchup: **Battling Bishops** vs. **Fighting Saints** in a tag-team match.

Colors

Tint City: In total, there are more than 200 schools with 16 hues, including those that are:
- Dark: Union College **Garnet Chargers** (Schenectady, NY)
- Fruitful: Syracuse **Orange** (Syracuse, NY)
- Immense: Dartmouth **Big Green** (Hanover, NH)
- Namely: Gustavus Adolphus **Golden Gusties** (St. Peter, MN)

- Quick: Saint Francis **Red Flash** (Loretto, PA)
- Royal: Wellesley College **Blue** (Wellesley, MA)
- Scary: McDaniel College **Green Terror** (Westminster, MD)
- Together: Indiana-Columbus **Crimson Pride** (Columbus, IN)
- Up a Sleeve: Evansville **Purple Aces** (Evansville, IN)

Bright Side: Gold is the most popular color in collegiate nicknames (more than 50 schools), with the **Golden Eagles** accounting for half of that total.

Other golden names include **Gold Nuggets**, **Gold Rush**, **Golden Bears**, **Golden Bulls**, **Golden Falcons**, **Golden Flashes**, **Golden Flyers**, **Golden Gophers**, **Golden Griffins**, **Golden Grizzlies**, **Golden Gusties**, **Golden Hurricane**, **Golden Knights**, **Golden Lions**, **Golden Norsemen**, **Golden Rams**, **Golden Suns**, **Golden Tigers**, **Golden Tornadoes**, and **Golden Wolves**.

Combatants

Soldiering On: War? What is it good for? Creating collegiate nicknames! Say it again! More than 170 schools have nicknames involving those who fight in battle. **Warriors**, **Knights**, **Cavaliers**, and **Lancers** lead the way, followed by nicknames that are:
- Artillerymen: Pratt Institute **Cannoneers** (Brooklyn, NY); Jefferson CC **Cannoneers** (Watertown, NY)
- Entertainers: Chabot College **Gladiators** (Hayward, CA)
- Heroic: Furman **Paladins** (Greenville, SC)
- Jewish: Yeshiva University **Maccabees** (New York, NY)

- Rebellious: George Washington University **Revolutionaries** (Washington, D.C.)
- Romans: Bucks County **Centurions** (Newtown, PA); Montcalm **Centurions** (Sidney, MI)
- Sandy: Imperial Valley **Desert Warriors** (Imperial, CA)
- Toxophilites: St. Louis CC **Archers** (Ferguson, MO)

Cougars

Cat's Meow: **Cougars** is the third-most popular collegiate nickname with almost 60 schools. The **Cougars**, **Panthers** (No. 5 most popular with 50+ schools), **Mountain Lions** (8), **Pumas** (4), and **Catamounts** (2) are all different names for the same cat – the species *Puma concolor*, which is native to North America and South America.

Name Game: Coach John Bender, whose face inspired Saint Louis University to be the **Billikens**, was also responsible for other nicknames. Bender coached the Washington State **Cougars** (on two separate occasions) and liked the nickname so much, he gave his club football team the moniker while teaching at the University of Houston. The school would eventually adopt the nickname officially in 1946.

He also named Kansas State the **Wildcats** when he was the head coach of the school in 1915. But after he left. another coach changed the name, before the university reverted to the **Wildcats** in 1920.

Dogs

Woofers: Colleges and universities love their dogs. Even some schools without canine nicknames find a way to have man's best friend roaming the sidelines, including Texas A&M (Reveille), Tennessee (Smokey), and Georgetown (Jack).

It's a dog-eat-dog world out there. And you get to pet these mascots – if you are wearing the correct school colors.

The most popular pooch is the **Bulldog**, with more than 50 schools choosing it as a nickname, followed by **Huskies** and **Greyhounds**. In total, there are almost 100 colleges and universities with dog nicknames representing 14 breeds, including those that are:
- Energetic: Pacific University **Boxers** (Forest Grove, OR)
- Fast: Gardner-Webb **Runnin' Bulldogs** (Boiling Springs, NC)
- Friendly: Maryland-Baltimore **Retrievers** (Baltimore, MD)
- Gigantic: Albany **Great Danes** (Albany, NY)
- Slender: Southern Illinois **Salukis** (Carbondale, IL)
- Smart: Spartanburg **Border Collies** (Spartanburg, SC)
- Trackers: John Jay College of Criminal Justice **Bloodhounds** (New York, NY)

Dream Matchup: **Boxers** vs. **Retrievers**: One packs a punch, but what happens when the other keeps returning it to them again and again? Whose bite is worse than their bark? The **Great Danes** will be there to ensure there is no cheating. The loser has to run laps with the **Runnin' Bulldogs**.

Eagles

Go Birds: The No. 1 collegiate nickname is the **Eagles**, with almost 90 schools opting for it as a nickname. And that doesn't count the different **Eagles** flying in several other entries, including those that are:
- Ascending: Elmira College **Soaring Eagles** (Elmira, NY)
- Flightless: Life University **Running Eagles** (Marietta, GA)
- Loud: Southern Indiana **Screaming Eagles** (Evansville, IN); Toccoa Falls **Screaming Eagles** (Toccoa, GA)
- Patriotic: Lock Haven **Bald Eagles** (Lock Haven, PA)
- Prized: **Golden Eagles** (25 schools)
- Violet: Niagara University **Purple Eagles** (Lewiston, NY)

Equines

Horsepower: More than 60 schools have chosen equine-related nicknames. **Mustangs** are the most popular, but there are other collegiate horses (and their cousins), including those that are:
- Alternative Spellings: Kentucky State **Thorobreds** and **Thorobredettes** (Frankfort, KY)
- Competitive: Murray State **Racers** (Murray, KY)
- Golden: Laredo College **Palominos** (Laredo, TX); Palo Alto **Palominos** (San Antonio, TX)
- Little: Panola College **Ponies** (Carthage, TX)
- Long Eared: Central Missouri **Jennies** (Warrensburg, MO)
- Speedy: Skidmore **Thoroughbreds** (Saratoga Springs, NY)

- Studs: Abraham Baldwin Agricultural **Stallions** (Tifton, GA); North American University **Stallions** (Stafford, TX)
- Three or Under: Panola College **Fillies** (Carthage, TX)
- Trains: Arkansas Hope-Texarkana **Iron Horses** (Hope, AR)

Felines

Out of the Bag: Cats rule the jungle of collegiate nicknames. The **Tigers**, **Cougars**, and **Panthers** each represent more than 50 schools, with **Lions** and **Wildcats** close by. All told, there are more than 325 schools with feline nicknames, including those that are:
- Airborne: SOWELA Technical **Flying Tigers** (Lake Charles, LA)
- Extinct: Marantha Baptist **Sabercats** (Watertown, WI)
- Glowing: Central New Mexico **Suncats** (Albuquerque, NM)
- Keynote: Kishwaukee **Kougars** (Malta, IL)
- Nocturnal: Schoolcraft College **Ocelots** (Livonia, MI)
- Players: Thiel College **Tomcats** (Greenville, PA)

Fictional

Reality Bites: Fabricated colleges have played significant roles in popular movies, television shows, and narratives – and some were given nicknames.

- Adams **Atoms** – *Revenge of the Nerds*
- Cadwallader University **Eagles** – *Fast Break*
- Eastern Colorado **Big Horns** – *The Last of Us*
- Eastern State **Timberwolves** – *The Program*
- Faber College **Mongols** – *National Lampoon's Animal House*
- Grand Lakes University **Hooters** – *Back to School*
- Greendale Community College **Human Beings** – *Community*
- Harrison University **Cougars** – *Old School*
- Hillman College **Falcons** – *A Different World*; *The Cosby Show*
- Hudson **Hawks** and **Huskies** – *Law & Order SVU*
- Minnesota State **Screaming Eagles** – *Coach*
- Miskatonic **Fighting Cephalopods** – *H.P. Lovecraft anthology*
- Penbrook **Penguins** – *Boy Meets World*
- Port Chester University **Cranes** – *PCU*
- Redwood State **Fighting Pinecones** – *Weeds*
- Springfield A&M **Snortin' Swine** – *The Simpsons*
- Springfield University **Nittany Tide** – *The Simpsons*
- South Central Louisiana State **Mud Dogs** – *The Waterboy*
- South Harmon Institute of Technology **Sandwiches** – *Accepted*
- Texas State **Armadillos** – *Necessary Roughness*
- Western University **Dolphins** – *Blue Chips*
- Wossamatta U **Mighty Moose Herd** – *The Adventures of Rocky & Bullwinkle*

Fighting

Knock Outs: Some schools sound like they are spoiling for a bar brawl. More than 25 colleges and universities advertise that they are prone to antagonize and battle via their nickname, including those that are:
- Brilliant: Rose-Hulman Institute of Technology **Fightin' Engineers** (Terre Haute, IN)
- Echoing: Muskingum College **Fighting Muskies** (New Concord, OH)
- Ghostly: Wisconsin-Baraboo Sauk County **Fighting Spirits** (Baraboo, WI)
- Hooty: Harford **Fighting Owls** (Bel Air, MD)
- Humpy: Campbell **Fighting Camels** (Buies Creek, NC)
- Spiny: Copper Mountain **Fighting Cacti** (Joshua Tree, CA)

Dream Matchup: **Fightin' Engineers** vs. **Fighting Cacti**. Zoom meetings or needles. Who can last the longest?

Fire

Burning Up: They didn't start the fire, but some colleges and universities want to let the world know their spirits are burning, including those that are:
- Blazing: Alverno **Inferno** (Milwaukee, WI)
- Flaming: **Flames** (6)
- Red-Hot: Southeastern University **Fire** (Lakeland, FL)
- Sweltering: Tennessee Southern **Firehawks** (Pulaski, TN)
- Turbulent: Arizona Christian **Firestorm** (Phoenix, AZ)

Flight

Fly Away: Three faculty members decided the University of Dayton needed a nickname in 1923. During a football game, their brainstorming eventually focused on honoring the hometown Wright brothers, who two decades prior had achieved flight. They considered several names, including Aviators and Kitty Hawks, before deciding on the **Flyers**. There are other flying nicknames, including those that are:
- Appropriate: Hope College **Flying Dutchmen** (Holland, MI)
- German: Lebanon Valley College **Flying Dutchmen** (Annville, PA)
- Royalty: Wayland Baptist **Flying Queens** (Plainview, TX)
- Winged: Lewis University **Flyers** (Romeoville, IL)
- Winged, Too: Sandhills CC **Flyers** (Pinehurst, NC)

Hawks

Free Birds: The **Hawks** are the eighth most popular collegiate nickname, with nearly 40 schools. That doesn't include the 29 other collegiate nicknames that include a variation of hawks: **Bayhawks, Black Hawks, Blackhawks, Blue Hawks, CityHawks, Crimson Hawks, Duhawks, Fighting Hawks, Firehawks, IceHawks, Jayhawks, Kohawks, Lakehawks, Mountain Hawks, Night Hawks, Nighthawks, Red Hawks, Redhawks, RedHawks, River Hawks, Riverhawks, RiverHawks, Scarlet Hawks, Seahawks, Skyhawks, Thunderhawks, V-Hawks, War Hawks**, and **Warhawks**.

Heritage

Legacy: Many nicknames represent groups who share a common ancestry, homeland, religion, or cultural heritage. Scotland is the leader with **Scots** (7), **Highlanders** (7), **Fighting Scots** (4), and a few others. All told, more than 50 schools are using those types of nicknames, including those that are:

- Early: Albion College **Britons** (Albion, MI)
- English: New England College **Pilgrims** (Henniker, New Hampshire)
- Friends: **Quakers** (4)
- Gaelic: St. Mary's **Gaels** (Moraga, CA); Iona **Gaels** (New Rochelle, NY)
- Indo-Europeans: Carlow University **Celtics** (Pittsburgh, PA); St. Thomas **Celts** (Houston, TX)
- Lone Starred: South Plains **Texans** (Levelland, TX); Tarleton State **Texans** (Stephenville, TX)
- Louisiana Acadians: Louisiana-Lafayette **Ragin' Cajuns** (Lafayette, LA)
- Netherlanders: Central College **Dutch** (Pella, IA)
- Saxony: Alfred **Saxons** (Alfred, NY)
- Scandinavian: Northeastern Oklahoma A&M **Golden Norsemen** (Miami, OK); North Hennepin **Norsemen** (Brooklyn Park, MN); **Norse** (4)
- Scottish: Sinclair **Tartans** (Dayton, OH); Carnegie Mellon **Tartans** (Pittsburgh, PA);
- Texans of Mexican Descent: El Paso CC **Tejanos** (El Paso, Texas)

Gators

See You Later: The **Gators** nickname is used by 10 schools, including the University of Florida (Gainesville, FL). In 1907, a drugstore owner from Gainesville visited his son at the University of Virginia. As part of the visit, the duo went to the Michie

Company to purchase banners and pennants in the colors of the University of Florida. The pair was asked what emblem should be used in conjunction with the school's name, since it didn't have a nickname. That's when the son, Austin Miller, offered the name "Alligators," because they were native to the state. The only problem was that the Michie artist had never seen an alligator. Austin hurried to the Virginia library, where he found a suitable picture of an alligator. The Florida Alligator banners and pennants were a big hit with students in 1908, eventually gaining in popularity across the campus. In 1911, the Florida nickname officially became the **Gators**.

Lawbreakers

Caught Stealing: Criminals of both the land and sea have inspired collegiate nicknames, with **Pirates**, **Buccaneers**, and **Raiders** leading the way. In all, there are 60 schools whose nicknames are on the wrong side of the law, including those that are:
- Cattle Thieves: Central Wyoming **Rustlers** (Riverton, WY); Golden West **Rustlers** (Huntington Beach, CA)
- Outlaws: Clatsop CC **Bandits** (Astoria, OR)
- Plunderers: Arkansas-Batesville **River Bandits** (Batesville, AR)
- Rogues: Bakersfield **Renegades** (Bakersfield, CA); Columbia College **Renegades** (Chicago, IL); Ohlone **Renegades** (Fremont, CA)

Marine Animals

Hook, Line & Sinker: Aquatic animals are not popular collegiate nicknames, with only around 30 schools. **Dolphins** and **Sharks** are the most prevalent, but there are other sea creatures, including those that are:
- Accelerated: Palm Beach Atlantic **Sailfish** (West Palm Beach, FL)
- Black & Whites: Whatcom CC **Orcas** (Bellingham, WA)
- Flattened: Coastal Pines Technical **Stingrays** (Waycross, GA)
- Herbivores: State College of Florida, Manatee-Sarasota **Manatees** (Manatee, FL)
- Long-Nosed: Virginia Wesleyan **Marlins** (Norfolk, VA)
- Toothy: The New School **Narwhals** (New York, NY)

- Sea Level: There are more than 15 schools with "Sea" in the nickname, including **Sea Aggies, Sea Beggars, Sea Devils, Sea Gulls, Sea Lions, Seahawks, Seawolves,** and **SeaWolves**.

Mythology and Folklore

Pandora's Box: The legends of ancient Greece are prevalent when it comes to collegiate nicknames. The **Spartans**, **Trojans**, and **Titans** are the most popular, but some schools have gone in other directions for their mythological and legendary nicknames, including those that are:
- Abominable: Cleveland CC **Yetis** (Shelby, NC)
- Guardians: A dragon known as a wyvern is said to protect Worcestershire, England, making it a fitting nickname for a school based in Worcester, Massachusetts – the Quinsigamond CC **Wyverns**.
- Impish: The Trinity Christian **Trolls** (Palo Heights, IL) name comes from the legend of a small creature said to guard the golf course where the college now stands.
- Jason's Backup Dancers: **Argonauts** (3)
- Norse: Carteret CC **Kraken** (Morehead City, NC)
- Smoldering: The Hawaii-Hilo **Vulcans** (Hilo, Hawaii) and the PennWest California **Vulcans** (California, PA) both pay homage to Vulcan, a Roman god of fire and volcanoes, not to Captain Kirk's science officer onboard the USS Enterprise.
- Watery: Atlantis University **Atlanteans** (Miami, FL)

- Wise: The Claremont-Mudd-Scripps **Athenas** (Claremont, CA) and the Mount St. Mary's **Athenians** (Los Angeles, CA) both honor Athena, the Greek goddess of wisdom and courage.
- Women: Converse **Valkyries** (Spartanburg, SC)

Dream Matchup: **Atlanteans** vs **Kraken**. You would need an underwater camera; otherwise, it would be a lot of loud splashing, which would get boring quickly.

Native American

Indigenous: Native American-associated nicknames currently in use by colleges or universities include:
- Cochise College **Apaches** (Douglas, AZ): Tyler Junior College **Apaches** (Tyler, TX)
- Pima CC **Aztecs** (Tucson, AZ); San Diego State **Aztecs** (San Diego, CA)
- Black Hawk **Braves** (Kewanee, IL); North Carolina at Pembroke **Braves** (Pembroke, NC)
- Waubonsee **Chiefs** (Sugar Grove, IL)
- Haskell Indian Nations **Fighting Indians** (Lawrence, KS)
- Chipola College **Indians** (Marianna, FL); Itawamba CC **Indians** (Fulton, MS); McCook CC **Indians** (McCook, NE); South Carolina-Salkehatchie **Indians** (Allendale, SC)

Some schools have received support from tribes to keep their nicknames: Catawba College **Catawba Indians** (Salisbury, NC); Central Michigan **Chippewas** (Mount Pleasant, MI); Florida State

Seminoles (Tallahassee, FL); Mississippi College **Choctaws** (Clinton, MS); and Utah **Utes** (Salt Lake City, UT).

Since the late 1980s, more than 50 colleges and universities have changed their Native American-associated nicknames or removed references to Native American culture from their athletic programs or game day presentations.

North America

Border Lines: The following are some other North American colleges and universities with nicknames:

Canada
- Acadia University **Axemen** (Wolfville, NS)
- Toronto Metropolitan University **Bold** (Toronto, ON)
- Cégep André-Laurendeau **Boomerang** (Montreal, QC)
- Fraser Valley **Cascades** (Abbotsford, BC)
- Trent University **Excalibur** (Peterborough, ON)
- Alberta **Golden Bears** and **Pandas** (Edmonton, AB)
- Northern Alberta Institute of Technology **Ooks** (Edmonton, AB) – short for Ookpik, a snowy owl
- Université du Québec ETS **Piranhas** (Montreal, QC)
- Great Plains College **SunDogs** (Swift Current, SK)
- Winnipeg **Wesmen** (Winnipeg, MB)
- St. Francis Xavier University **X-Men** and **X-Women** (Antigonish, NS)

Mexico
- Universidad de Guanajuato **Abejas** (Guanajuato City, Gto.) – *Bees*
- Instituto Politécnico Nacional **Burros Blancas** (Mexico City, CDMX) – *White Donkeys*
- Universidad Autónoma de Tamaulipas **Correcaminos** (Ciudad Victoria, Tamps.) – *Roadrunners*
- Universidad Autónoma de Guadalajara **Gansos Salvajes** (Guadalajara, Jal.) – *Wild Geese*
- Instituto Tecnológico Autónomo de México (ITAM) **Itamitas** (Mexico City, CDMX) – *Students of ITAM*
- Universidad de Colima **Loros** (Colima, Col.) – *Parrots*
- Universidad Autónoma de Chapingo **Toros Salvajes** (Texcoco, Méx.) – *Wild Bulls*
- Universidad de Quintana Roo **Toucans** (Chetumal, Q.R.)

Occupations

Working for the Weekend: Most students attend college to acquire the knowledge and skills necessary for a career. Some jobs are already in the schools' nicknames, including those that are:
- Beer Makers: Vassar College **Brewers** (Poughkeepsie, NY); Williamsburg Technical **Brewers** (Kingstree, SC)
- Bosses: St. Clair County **Skippers** (Port Huron, MI)
- Catchers: Northwest College **Trappers** (Powell, WY)
- Commanders: Christopher Newport University **Captains** (Newport News, VA)
- Directors: Goodwin University **Navigators** (East Hartford, CT)

- Envoys: Franklin & Marshall College **Diplomats** (Lancaster, PA)
- Leaders: Washington & Jefferson College **Presidents** (Washington, PA)
- Pilots: Arkansas State-Newport **Aviators** (Newport, AR)
- Quiet: Saint Joseph's College of Maine **Monks** (Standish, ME)
- Sorcerers: LeMoyne-Owen **Magicians** (Memphis, TN)
- Technicians: Williams College of Trade **Mechanics** (Media, PA)

Plants

Put Down Roots: Oak trees are the most popular plants in collegiate nicknames, with **Mighty Oaks** (3) and **Oaks** (2) leading the way. There are other flora nicknames, including those that are:
- Abundant: Goshen College **Maple Leafs** (Goshen, IN)
- Expansive: New College of Florida **Mighty Banyans** (Sarasota, FL)
- Fiber: Arkansas-Monticello **Cotton Blossoms** (Monticello, AR)

- Huge: Indiana State **Sycamores** (Terre Haute, IN)
- Spirally: Chaminade **Silverswords** (Honolulu, HI)

Into the Woods: There are also collegiate nicknames for those whose job it is to take down trees, including the **Lumberjacks** (6), **Loggers** (2), **Foresters** (2), and the Gray Harbor College **Chokers** (Aberdeen, WA).

Reptiles

Snake Eyes: There are more than 25 schools that have a reptile nickname, with **Gators** being the most popular, followed by **Rattlers** and **Cobras**. Other collegiate reptilians include those that are:
- Ambush Predators: Hostos College **Caimans** (Bronx, NY)
- Scaly: Truckee Meadows **Lizards** (Reno, NV)
- Sticky: GateWay **Geckos** (Phoenix, AZ)
- Swimmers: Maryland **Terrapins** (College Park, MD)
- Venomous: Eastern Arizona **Gila Monsters** (Thatcher, AZ)
- Vipers: Florida Southern **Moccasins** (Lakeland, FL)

School Names

Say Again: Close to 20 schools (6 in Minnesota) did not have to go far to pick a nickname. The name was already spelled out for them, including those that are:
- Recurring: Augsburg University **Auggies** (Minneapolis, MN)
- Repeated: College of Saint Benedict **Bennies** (St. Joseph, MN)
- Repetitive: Immaculata University **Mighty Macs** (Chester, PA)

- Replayed: St. Thomas **Tommies** (Saint Paul, MN)
- Replays: Western Texas **Westerners** (Snyder, TX)
- Reruns: St. Olaf **Oles** (Northfield, MN)

Tigers

Feed the Kitty: With more than 60 schools, Tigers is the second-most popular collegiate nickname. Some Tigers include:

- The Auburn **Tigers** (Auburn, AL) nickname comes from a line in Oliver Goldsmith's poem *The Deserted Village* – "where crouching tigers await their hapless prey."
- When Auburn graduate Walter Riggs started the football program at Clemson University (Clemson, SC), he named the team the **Tigers**, like his alma mater.
- The LSU **Tigers** (Baton Rouge, LA) nickname can be traced back to Louisiana military units of the Civil War, which used the Tigers name.
- A militia known as the Missouri Tigers, which protected the town of Columbia from marauders in 1864, is where the Missouri **Tigers** (Columbia, MO) gets its nickname from.
- Princeton University (Princeton, NJ) was the first to adopt the name after sportswriters referred to the early 1880s football teams as the **Tigers** because their jerseys and socks were orange with black stripes.
- Trinity University (San Antonio, TX) takes its nickname from when it was located in Waxahachie, Texas. In 1916, the Detroit Tigers held spring training near the school, and students began referring to themselves as **Tigers**.

Top Collegiate Nicknames

1. Eagles - 87
2. Tigers - 62
3. Cougars - 59
4. Bulldogs - 56
5. Panthers - 52
6. Warriors - 46
7. Lions - 44
8. Hawks - 40
9. Wildcats - 37
10. Pioneers - 36
11t. Falcons - 35
11t. Knights - 35
13. Bears - 33
14. Vikings - 32
15. Rams - 29
16. Saints - 27

Trojans

Underdogs: There are more than 20 schools with the nickname **Trojans**, including the University of Southern California (Los Angeles, CA). *Los Angeles Times* sports editor Owen Bird gets credit for that nickname choice after being asked by the Southern California athletic director to come up with something in 1912. Bird said he chose the **Trojans** because, at the time, USC was constantly competing against bigger and better-equipped teams, yet still maintained a fighting spirit reminiscent of the Trojans of Greek mythology.

Weather

Rain or Shine: The **Storm** is the most popular weather-related nickname which does not even include the Southwestern Illinois **Blue Storm** (Belleville, IL), Southern Nazarene **Crimson Storm** (Bethany, OK), St. John's **Red Storm** (New York, NY), University of Rio Grande **RedStorm** (Rio Grande, OH), or the Southeastern Oklahoma State **Savage Storm** (Durant, OK). Other weather names include **Cyclones**, **Hurricanes**, **Thunder**, and weather events that are:

- Extratropical: University of New England **Nor'easters** (Biddeford, Maine)
- Expensive: Geneva **Golden Tornadoes** (Beaver Falls, PA)
- Landlocked: Tulsa **Golden Hurricane** (Tulsa, OK)
- Solo: King University **Tornado** (Bristol, TN)
- Windy: Texas A&M International **Dustdevils** (Laredo, TX)

Wildcats

Fighting Words: **Wildcats** is the ninth most popular collegiate nickname, with almost 40 schools. Some reasons for a few of the collegiate **Wildcats** include:

- A commandant praised the Kentucky (Lexington, KY) football team at a chapel service after a win over Illinois in 1909, saying that they had "fought like wildcats." The name caught on.
- An impressed *Los Angeles Times* columnist said the University of Arizona (Tucson, AZ) football team had "showed the fight of wildcats" in a game against Occidental College in 1914. The name caught on.
- Sportswriter Wallace Abbey of the *Chicago Tribune* said the Northwestern University football team had "fought like wildcats" after a loss to the University of Chicago **Maroons** in 1924. The name caught on.
- A student who was a big fan of the Northwestern **Wildcats** nominated the same nickname for Cal State Chico (Chico, CA) in 1926. The name caught on.
- Bethune-Cookman University (Daytona Beach, FL) founder Dr. Mary Bethune watched the football team practice in 1923. She addressed the squad afterward and said, "You are ferocious. I dub thee the **Wildcats**." The name caught on.
- Football coaching assistant Edward Hunsinger suggested the **Wildcats** as a nickname for Villanova University (Philadelphia, PA) in 1926. The name caught on. However, his feelings toward fighting felines or their ferocity are not known.

Wolverines

War Veterans: There are no wolverines in the state of Michigan. The animal has never been trapped there, and the only verified sighting of a wild wolverine inside its borders occurred in 2004. There are multiple theories as to why it became known as the Wolverine State, including the trading of wolverine pelts at the Canadian border and the behavior of French trappers who acted like wild animals.

The most notable involves a boundary dispute in 1803 between Michigan and Ohio, known as the Toledo War. The Ohioans called the Michiganders "wolverines" because of their perceived terrible manners and incredible aggressiveness. The Michiganders thought the name complemented their tenacity and strength. Michigan was known as the Wolverine State from then on, with the University of Michigan (Ann Arbor, MI) adopting **Wolverines** as a nickname soon after its founding.

Same Name: There are six other schools with the **Wolverines** nickname. Wild wolverines have never been near those campuses either. Nor has Hugh Jackman.
- Essex County College (Newark, NJ)
- Grove City College (Grove City, PA)
- Morris Brown College (Atlanta, GA)
- San Bernardino Valley College (CA)
- Sierra College (Rocklin, CA)
- Utah Valley University (Orem, UT)

Part III: The States & D.C.

Collegiate nicknames, mascots, traditions, and other tidbits from the 50 states and Washington, D.C.

Alabama

Chowing Down: In 1916, Howard College (Birmingham) realized that having the same **Tigers** nickname as Auburn was not a positive. So the school held a vote to pick a new identity: Crimson Bulldogs or Baptist Bears. The Bulldogs crushed the Bears, partly because the students felt a bulldog could eat more of the Birmingham-Southern Panther – apparently prioritizing a possible fight between mascots over everything else.

The "Crimson" descriptor eventually was forgotten – probably because **Crimson Bulldogs** sounded like they needed to see a vet – leaving just the **Bulldogs**. Howard College became Samford University in 1965.

Memory Lane: The Alabama **Crimson Tide** (Tuscaloosa) became connected with elephants thanks to sportswriter Everett Strupper of the *Atlanta Journal*. He compared the Crimson Tide's blocking to that of the enormous animals in his story on the 1930 Alabama-Mississippi game, and the description caught on.

In the 1940s, the school had a live elephant named Alamite on campus for game days. But it wasn't until the 1979 Sugar Bowl that the costumed elephant known as Big Al became the official Alabama mascot.

Power Up: In 1969, the University of Alabama in Huntsville (UAH) needed a nickname for its brand-new basketball team. A history professor suggested Uhlans – a type of European cavalry armed with lances. Students thought it was edgy and unique; administrators thought it was asking to be laughed out of every gym in the South.

So, in a moment of "we need to fix this before it gets weird," the Director of Student Affairs slapped on Chargers. Why? Because horses charge, and Huntsville is in the Tennessee Valley, where a ton of electricity is generated – boom: **Uhlan Chargers**. Medieval cavalry meets the power company. Unsurprisingly, the Uhlan part didn't stick. Before long, it was just the **Chargers**, which did not require a history lesson before tipoff.

Rolling Deep: Toomer's Corner marks the line between downtown Auburn and the university campus, named after Toomer's Drugs, which has been there since 1896. Back in the day, it was the only place with a telegraph, so it was the spot to find out how the **Tigers** were doing on the road and celebrate a win.

Fast-forward to 1972: Auburn headed to Birmingham to face second-ranked Alabama. Tiger halfback Terry Henley confidently declared, "We're going to beat the No. 2 out of Alabama." Down 16–3, the **Tigers** blocked two punts and returned them both for touchdowns in the final six minutes, winning 17–16 in what became forever known as the Punt Bama Punt game.

Auburn fans raced to Toomer's Corner to celebrate, remembered Henley's comment, and brought along toilet paper for emphasis. The oak trees never stood a chance, and Rolling Toomer's Corner was born. Even after the original trees were poisoned and removed in 2013, the TP-tossing tradition lives on.

Setting Sun: The Faulkner State Community College **Sun Chiefs** (Bay Minette) faded away after the school merged into Coastal Alabama Community College.

Take Flight: The Auburn **Tigers** have had an eagle as part of the football program for more than a century, which today involves the "War Eagle" battle cry and a bird soaring over the field.

How "War Eagle" came to be has multiple theories, including one involving a Civil War soldier bringing his pet eagle to a game against Georgia in 1892 and another where Auburn fans adopted the battle cry of the Saxons, who had bestowed the name on the buzzards who followed them from battle to battle to feast on the dead warriors.

Another possibility is the 1912 Auburn football player who liked to yell "War Eagle" before, during, and after games for no particular reason, which caught on with fans, possibly out of fear.

Teacher's Pets: The Athens College **Collegians** (Athens) are now the Athens State **Bears**.

Turtle-Dovin': Country band Alabama dropped *Dixieland Delight* in January 1983 – just two days after the passing of Bear Bryant, the **Crimson Tide**'s legendary coach. The song shot to No. 1 on the *Billboard* country chart before eventually sliding into Alabama football games as a fun sing-along. That is, until fans started adding some very not-so-family-friendly jabs at Auburn, LSU, and Tennessee.

By 2015, the school had to ban the tune altogether, basically grounding those rowdy ne'er-do-wells in attendance. It came back in 2018, but only after administrators begged everyone to please act like their grandmas were listening. Meanwhile, Tennessee fans love pointing out the song name-checks their state multiple times, which, during the Nick Saban era, many counted as a win.

Wave Off: In 1922, Troy University ditched its old nicknames – the **Bulldogs** and the **Teachers** – and went with **Trojans**. That lasted until football coach Albert Elmore rolled into town. Elmore, a proud Alabama **Crimson Tide** alum, basically said, "This team name is now going to be whatever reminds me of my college glory days." So, Troy obediently rebranded to the **Red Wave**, because apparently, in the 1930s, coaches didn't just call plays – they called school identities.

After four decades, students realized they no longer had to let a long-gone coach bully them. A quick vote – hours before a football game – brought back the **Trojans** in 1973.

Alaska

Bear Necessities: The **Nanooks** of the University of Alaska Fairbanks are derived from the Inuit word nanuq, which means "polar bear."

Bread Winner: The University of Alaska-Anchorage (UAA) was once the **Sourdoughs** – an honorific for veteran Alaskans who were tough enough to survive the rugged terrain and smart enough to keep a yeast starter alive in subzero weather. Early gold prospectors depended on sourdough for food, proving that sometimes the best way to strike it rich is to do it with the carbs.

Eventually, students and alumni grew tired of being called leavened bread. So UAA basketball Coach Bob Rachal went looking for a new nickname in 1977. He found the **Seawolves** via Wasgo the Sea Wolf, a myth from Alaskan native cultures.

The story is about a young man who traps the creature Wasgo, wears its fur, and gains superpowers. Then his mother-in-law dies of shame. She is not included on the school's logo.

Clubbed: The Sheldon Jackson College **Golden Seals** no longer exist. The school closed due to declining enrollment in 2007.

Arizona

Bright Spot: A student election made the **Sun Devils** the nickname of Arizona State (Tempe), replacing the **Bulldogs** in 1946.

Flying High: The Mesa Community College **Thunderbirds** were once known as the **Hokams**, a prehistoric people who lived in present-day Arizona.

Roughin' It: The Yavapai College **Roughriders** (Prescott) take their name from the volunteer regiment formed in 1898 after the sinking of the USS Maine. The unit, eventually led by future U.S. President Teddy Roosevelt, was known as the Rough Riders and fought in the Spanish-American War. The group first trained at the Arizona Territory's Ft. Whipple, right where Yavapai's campus now sits.

Stormy Weather: Tohono O'odham Community College (Sells) is the **Jegos**, pronounced "jug-ohs" – an O'odham word for the dust storms that roll in with the monsoon rains. It's a nickname that captures both the power of the desert and the certainty that you'll be brushing sand out of your teeth afterward.

Arkansas

Bootleggers: The Phillips Community College **Ridge Runners** (Helena-West Helena) refer to the folks who lived high up in the mountains and ran the ridges to avoid deputy sheriffs while carrying illegal moonshine.

Fiery: The East Arkansas **Delta Dragons** (Forrest City) are the only school in the country with that nickname.

Name Game: Arkansas State (Jonesboro) has had trouble deciding on a nickname. For a while, it was the **Aggies**, then **Farmers**, then **Gorillas**, then **Warriors**. In 1931, the nickname officially became the **Indians** until it was replaced by the **Red Wolves** in 2008.

Paper Trails: Called the best technical foul in sports, John Brown University (Siloam Springs) students celebrate their team's first basket of the home season by tossing thousands of rolls of toilet paper onto the court. The tradition started in the 1970s when a few rogue **Golden Eagle** fans decided a game needed more bathroom supplies. Today, over 2,500 fans chunk some Charmin in a synchronized blizzard of two-ply glory.

Yes, it's a technical foul, and yes, it takes some time to clean up – but even the opposing coaches and players admit it's awesome. And it works: Since 2000, the **Golden Eagles** have only lost one Toilet Paper Game. Turns out the secret to winning basketball might just be wiping the floor with your opponents.

Pluralize: The Harding University **Bisons** (yes, with an s) is one of only two schools bold enough to tell grammar to take a hike and stand on how some people apparently referred to multiple bison in the 1920s. In the mid-1990s, the school tried to drop the rogue "s," rolling out new signs, cheers, and cheerleader uniforms that all referenced Bison.

But fans weren't having it. So, after a short-lived experiment in linguistic correctness, the administration quietly gave up and let the **Bisons** live on. Today, Harding (Searcy) remains proudly plural – proving that sometimes, tradition beats grammar, and spellcheck can go kick rocks.

Seeing Red: In 1908, Henderson College - now Henderson State - (Arkadelphia) held a contest to name its football team. Nellie Hartsgeld won with **Red Jackets**, inspired by the team's red jerseys. Cute idea – but people quickly ignored it by just calling them the Red Men or the Reds, because apparently creativity wasn't a thing in the early 1900s. By 1912, a new nickname started floating around: **Reddies**.

Nobody's exactly sure why, but one popular theory is that **Reddies** was easier to squeeze into pep songs and yells. Which makes sense – "Fight, fight, you Red Jackets!" doesn't exactly roll off the tongue, and "Go Reds!" sounds like you accidentally wandered into a baseball game.

So, the **Reddies** stuck – proof that sometimes your mascot destiny is decided not by history, but by rhyme scheme.

Stubborn: The Southern Arkansas University **Muleriders** (Magnolia) nickname comes from the early 1900s when the school was known as the Third District Agricultural School (TDAS). In

1912, several TDAS football players rode mules a few miles to see football Coach George Turrentine to discuss the previous season.

There were only four cars in the county, and none of them were accessible to them. When the players arrived, Coach Turrentine gave a greeting of "My mule riders!"

His ode to harnessing the power of stubborn livestock soon became the school's nickname.

California

Above It All: In 1954, UC Riverside students got to vote on a school nickname. The options? Rocks, Tigers, and Aphids. (Yes, apparently someone thought "Go Aphids!" would strike fear into opponents, or at least into local farmers.)

The winner was **Hylanders**, chosen because the campus was higher than the rest of the town. Topographical smugness for the win! Later, the spelling was changed to **Highlanders**, which opened the door for Scottish culture like bagpipes and kilts, but probably not haggis.

Ahoy Matey: The Santa Monica College **Corsairs** honor those French-backed privateers who plundered enemy ships – basically pirates with a permission slip. And if you're stealing for France, you're not wasting time on cheap rum and hardtack. You're getting the good stuff.

Why did Santa Monica pick the **Corsairs**? Nobody really knows. The best guess is: "Well, we're near the ocean. Boats exist. Sure, why not?" It's the kind of mascot logic that happens when a committee meeting runs too long.

Meanwhile, the College of the Redwoods (Eureka) decided that glorifying nautical banditry wasn't the best look, so they recently retired the **Corsairs** for something more wholesome: **Redwoods** – same name, but this time with more feeling and extra sincerity.

Big Bad Wolves: For almost a century, Compton College was the **Tartars**, named after Mongolian warriors – because nothing says Southern California quite like 13th-century marauders.

But in 2025, the school changed to something closer to home, the **Coyotes**, an animal that, unlike a Mongol cavalry, shows up on campus from time to time.

Galloping Through: The University of Southern California **Trojans** have had a white horse named Traveler ridden around the Los Angeles Memorial Coliseum by someone in a warrior costume at home football games since 1961. The first rider dressed in the outfit that actor Charlton Heston wore in the movie *Ben-Hur*.

Hit the Road: UC Santa Barbara didn't always have the suave, swashbuckling **Gauchos.** Back when it was Santa Barbara State, the teams were called the **Roadrunners**.

Enter football Coach Spud Harder (his actual name, not a potato superhero). Spud decided the spindly bird wasn't intimidating enough and demanded a change, so the students held an election for a new nickname in 1936.

Thanks to the coed vote, the school went Hollywood, choosing the **Gauchos** after Douglas Fairbanks' brooding, mustache-twirling performance in the movie *The Gaucho,* giving UCSB athletes a mascot who could ride a horse, swing a sword, and smolder at the camera – all at the same time.

Horsin' Around: Santa Clara University finally saddled up as the **Broncos** in 1923. Before that, the school's students were known as the **Mission Lads**, **Missionites**, **Friars**, and **Prunepickers**, for the area's fruit industry.

Send Up: The Stanford (Palo Alto) band's quest to spoof college mascots led them to consider The Steaming Manhole Cover and the French Fry. Ultimately, they went arboreal, unveiling the Stanford Tree at halftime of a 1975 football game against California, Berkeley.

Stanford students now compete to be the unofficial mascot by performing stunts during Tree Week, designing a new Tree costume each year, and preparing to make a whole lot of money after graduation.

Versed: The Whittier College **Poets** (Whittier) are named after Quaker poet and abolitionist John Greenleaf Whittier. The school decided that literary brilliance beats ferocity – because nothing intimidates opponents like iambic pentameter.

Wet Blanket: The St. Ignatius **Gray Fog** is now the University of San Francisco **Dons**.

Colorado

Bird's Eye View: In 1955, the first graduating class of the U.S. Air Force Academy (Colorado Springs) selected the **Falcons** as the school's official mascot for its speed, courage, and powerful flight.

They did not specify a specific type of falcon, so any falcon species native to North America – the gyrfalcon, peregrine, prairie, merlin, or kestrel – can be an Academy mascot. The first mascot was a peregrine falcon named Mach 1.

Boom: The Colorado School of Mines (Golden) has a miniature burro named Blaster that sprints across the field after every **Orediggers** touchdown.

Don't let the miniature part fool you – the little donkey hauls some serious school spirit. The name came from a campus contest, which a chemistry professor fittingly won.

Collegiate Bands

- **All-American Marching Band** - Purdue
- **Aristocrat of Bands** - Tennessee State
- **Bullet Marching Band** - Gettysburg
- **Diamond Marching Band** - Temple
- **Fightin' Texas Aggie Band** - Texas A&M
- **Fire of the Carolinas Marching Band** - Elon
- **Goin' Band from Raiderland** - Texas Tech
- **Golden Wave Band** - Baylor
- **Good Time Marching Band** - Holy Cross
- **Governor's Own Marching Band** - Austin Peay
- **Herd of Thunder** - South Florida
- **Human Jukebox** - Southern University
- **Magnificent Marching Machine** - Morgan State
- **Marching 100** - Florida A&M
- **Marching 101** - South Carolina State
- **Marching Force** - Hampton
- **Marching Mizzou** - Missouri
- **Marching Musical Machine of the Mid-South (M4)** - Arkansas-Pine Bluff
- **Marching Owls** - Florida Atlantic
- **Marching Pirates** - East Carolina
- **Marching Sound Machine** - North Carolina Central
- **Marching Southerners** - Jacksonville State
- **Marching Storm** - Prairie View A&M

- **Maverick Machine** - Minnesota State
- **Mean Green Marching Machine** - Miss. Valley State
- **Mighty Marching Hornets** - Alabama State
- **Mighty Sound of the South** - Memphis
- **Million Dollar Band** - Alabama
- **Ocean of Soul** - Texas Southern
- **Power Sound of the South** - North Carolina State
- **Pride of Acadiana** - Louisiana-Lafayette
- **Pride of the Rockies** - Northern Colorado
- **Pride of the South** - Mississippi
- **Pride of the Southland Band** - Tennessee
- **Pride of the Sunshine** - Florida
- **Redcoat Marching Band** - Georgia
- **Showtime Marching Band** - Howard
- **Sonic Boom of the South** - Jackson State
- **Sound & the Fury -** Tarleton State
- **Sound of the Natural State** - Arkansas State
- **Sound of the Sandhills** - Campbell
- **Sounds of Dyn-O-Mite** - Alcorn State
- **Spirit of Gold Marching Band** - Vanderbilt
- **Spirit of Southland** - Southeastern Louisiana
- **Star of Nevada** - Nevada-Las Vegas
- **Star of Northwest Ohio** - Ohio Northern
- **Thunder of the East** - Buffalo
- **Trojan Marching Band** - Southern California
- **Western Thunder Marching Band** - Wyoming

Buffalo Roam: After cycling through the **Arapahoes**, **Big Horns**, **Frontiersmen**, **Grizzlies**, and **Silver Helmets**, the University of Colorado (Boulder) held a contest for something better in 1934. The $5 prize went to the suggestion of **Buffaloes**, which started the tradition of having a live bison on the sideline for home football games.

In 1966, a bison calf was donated to the school, which students named Rraalph. Theories as to why include the junior class president was named Ralph, or they wanted to commemorate the sound of throwing up after partying too much. The name was changed to Ralphie in 1967, and since then, six female North American bison have led the team onto the field.

Graceful: The Lamar Community College **Runnin' Lopes** (Lamar) is one of two U.S. schools that shorten "antelope" in its nickname.

Ramming Speed: In 1945, Colorado A&M students decided that **Aggies** just wasn't cutting it anymore as a nickname. So they held a vote and picked the **Rams** – because animals that run headfirst into things on purpose are fun to cheer for.

Of course, change takes time, so for years the school went by the awkward hybrid **Aggie Rams**, which sounds less like a nickname and more like a weird square dance routine.

By 1954, they had their first live mascot: CAM the Ram (named after the school's acronym). CAM has always been a Rambouillet sheep – fancy wool, French origins, and a face that says, "I will absolutely headbutt your car." The school became Colorado State University in 1957, but opted not to change the mascot's name to the new acronym.

Connecticut

Bear in Mind: The U.S. Coast Guard Academy (New London) picked the Black Bear as its mascot in 1926 because bears are tenacious, and because of the Revenue Cutter Bear, a ship with a heroic crew that saved lives off the Alaskan coast. The nickname was simplified to **Bears**.

Cadets took it a step further by bringing a live cub to campus. She was named Objee, short for "objectionable presence," which tells you everything about what it's like to share a dorm with a bear. Over the years, there were 31 live Objees, the last leaving campus in 1984. During that time, Objee dined in the cadet wardroom, wrestled with cadets, and even joined them in the showers.

Desert Steed: When Connecticut College (New London) went co-ed in 1969, the new men on campus wanted a school basketball team. This presented two problems – they needed a coach and a nickname. Enter Mike Shenault, head of the school's print shop and mailroom, who had coached basketball in the Navy. Shenault also decided he'd handle the nickname business himself. He drew inspiration from animals he had seen while in the Middle East, praising their endurance, determination, and strength, and named the team the **Camels**.

Going Stag: Fairfield University kicked off its sports program in the 1940s with a cross-country team called the **Men in Red**, which sounds less like a college squad and more like a Cold War TV series with a lot of spies looking for microfilm.

By 1948, with baseball on the scene, the school held an election for a proper nickname. Students chose **Stags**, partly because Fairfield was in the Hartford Diocese and "hart" means a male red deer. So, in short, a pun won the day.

Yardbirds: Trinity College (Hartford) didn't have a nickname until 1899, when alumnus Joseph Buffington delivered a barnyard-themed speech at a regional Princeton Alumni Association dinner. He declared Princeton, Harvard, and Yale the big animals of the collegiate farm while Trinity was just a proud little bantam (chicken), "not a whit abashed at your hugeness, [and] satisfied with himself and his own particular coop." Students and media loved the underdog energy, and the school soon embraced the **Bantams** as its official nickname.

Delaware

Bird in the Hand: The **Blue Hens** of the University of Delaware (Newark) is a nickname not found in any other state.

Shocking: The Goldey-Beacom College **Lightning** (Wilmington) didn't exactly begin with a bolt from the blue – it started as a good, old-fashioned turf war between two rival business colleges.

In 1886, H.S. Goldey founded Wilmington Commercial College (eventually becoming Goldey College). Then in 1900, one of his instructors, W.H. Beacom, decided, "You know what? I'll start my own school down the street. That'll show him." And he did. Just a few blocks away.

For decades, the two schools coexisted like estranged cousins: same sports, same practice fields, same game facilities, but refused to play against each other. (Apparently, it's easier to share a field for more than 30 years than shake hands after a loss.) The schools merged to form a single institution in 1951.

Florida

All that Jazz: Florida A&M's (Tallahassee) first teams in the early 1920s were known as the **Jazz Birds**, a nod to athletic director and football Coach Franz "Jazz" Byrd. President John Robert Edward Lee wasn't a fan and rebranded them the **Tigers** until the squad played Edward Waters College, who also happened to be the **Tigers**. Lee decided that two teams with the same nickname was too confusing, so he picked **Rattlers** as the new name. The reason for it is less apparent, but the most popular version suggests that when the site for the school was first cleared, the only things left standing were Palmetto trees and rattlesnakes.

Anchors Away: The Gulf Coast State College **Commodores** (Panama City) didn't pick their nickname out of the sea air. Students nominated names, and the high-ranking naval officers won out thanks to three localish connections: the school sits on an old shipyard, there's a Navy base nearby, and, oddly enough, Vanderbilt University's **Commodores** are located exactly 500 miles away in Nashville. So basically, the logic was: Ships, sailors, and round numbers are neat!

Bird's the Word: In 1979, the University of North Florida (Jacksonville) needed a nickname and staged what became a "battle of the creatures." Students had their pick of Armadillos, Manatees, Seagulls, Sharks, Tadpoles, Coots, Pinecones, and Flashers (yes, really).

But professor Ray Bowen wasn't impressed – especially with the Seagulls, which he dismissed as "filthy birds." Bowen did his homework, found the osprey, and launched a write-in campaign with fliers praising the raptor's strength and elegance. The **Ospreys** soared past the competition, winning 47% of the vote, and then crushed the field in a follow-up election.

Do the Math: The New College of Florida (Sarasota) went from being the **Null Set**, a math term for a set with no elements or absolutely nothing, to the **Mighty Banyans**, towering trees that dot the campus. Students embraced the **Null Set** starting in 1997 because it felt perfectly in line with the school's progressive ethos, literally rallying behind nothing. However, in 2023, school trustees decided that 'nothing' wasn't much of a recruiting tool and voted to rebrand as the **Mighty Banyans**.

Eye of the Storm: The University of Miami (Coral Gables) became the **Hurricanes** after a monster storm flattened south Florida in 1926. The name was either suggested by a single football player to a reporter or voted on by the 1927 team, meaning the rest of the student body's name ideas got steamrolled by a Category 5 branding decision.

The school's mascot, Sebastian the Ibis, is rooted in the legend that the ibis is the last bird to leave before a hurricane and the first to return afterward. In 1957, residents of San Sebastian Hall sponsored an ibis float in the homecoming parade, and Miami's weatherproof waterfowl was born.

Hot Streak: Florida International University (University Park) started as the **Sunblazers** in 1973 – a nickname that sounded like either a heroic space crew or the world's most determined tanning salon. The school switched to the **Golden Panthers** in 1987, presumably because big cats are cooler and less likely to cause sunburn. In 2010, FIU decided to just be the **Panthers** like more than 50 other schools.

Making Change: In 1947, Florida State University (Tallahassee) students demanded a school nickname. An election was held, and

Seminoles defeated Statesmen, Rebels, Tarpons, Fighting Warriors, and Crackers.

Roll Call: Ave Maria University was founded in 1999 and picked a nickname straight out of boot camp. According to the school, **Gyrenes** is an old-school nickname the other military branches gave to Marines. It combines "GI" (government issue) with "Marine" to form "government issue Marine" or "Gyrene". Ave Maria adopted as a nickname, bringing the barracks to the Catholic liberal arts school.

Turf War: In 1962, Florida State professor Dean Coyle Moore told the **Seminole** players to "bring back some sod from between the hedges at Georgia." After FSU shocked the **Bulldogs** 18-0, team captain Gene McDowell dutifully ripped out a chunk of turf and took it home. Moore and Coach Bill Peterson buried it by the practice field, stuck a monument on top, and started a tradition: The Sod Cemetery.

Since then, FSU captains have returned with 113 chunks of real estate from against 40 different opponents. Games only qualify as "sod-worthy" if the **Seminoles** are an underdog, playing Florida, in a championship, a bowl, or if the head coach feels like it. The biggest tombstone contributors? Florida (14) and Miami (11). Southern Miss, Northern Illinois, and North Texas also have markers there proving that no blade of grass is safe from the Noles.

Workhorse: Florida State University (Tallahassee) has featured two living mascots since 1978: Chief Osceola in Seminole regalia – a male student with at least a 3.0 grade point average – riding Renegade, an Appaloosa horse, to the 50-yard line of Doak Campbell Stadium and dramatically planting a spear in the turf. No word on whether a student with a poor GPA is assigned the equally heroic task of following Renegade with a shovel and bucket.

Georgia

Bear With It: The first football game in the state of Georgia took place in 1892, when the Mercer University **Baptists** lost 50–0 to the University of Georgia **Bulldogs**.

Legend says that when one of Mercer's oversized linemen lumbered down the field, a Georgia fan asked loudly, "Whence cometh that bear?" which may be a fancy way of saying, "Big boy can't block us!"

The remark stuck with the Mercer faithful (apparently for decades), so when the school rebranded in 1924, the **Bears** won a school-wide election in a landslide.

Bug Out: The Georgia Tech **Yellow Jackets** (Atlanta) nickname is not derived from insects. It comes from fans wearing literal yellow jackets to games in the early 1900s, proving once again that college kids wearing coordinated outfits can change the world.

Fight Songs

- **Aggie War Hymn** - Texas A&M Aggies
- **Aggies Oh Aggies** - New Mexico State Aggies
- **All Hail to Kazoo** - Kalamazoo Hornets
- **Anchors Aweigh** - Navy Midshipmen
- **As the Backs Go Tearing By** - Dartmouth Big Green
- **Bear Down, Arizona** - Arizona Wildcats
- **Boomer Sooner** - Oklahoma Sooners
- **Bradley Loyalty Song** - Bradley Braves
- **Cheer Boys** - Jackson State Tigers
- **Chu, Chu, Rah, Rah** - Holy Cross Crusaders
- **Devils Gun** - Mississippi State Valley Delta Devils
- **Dynamite** - Vanderbilt Commodores
- **El 'C' Grande** - UC Santa Barbara Gauchos
- **Engineers Drinking Song** - MIT Engineers
- **Fight, Fight, Fight** - Colgate Raiders
- **Fight Team Fight** - Ball State Cardinals
- **Fyte Onne** - Albion College Britons
- **Give My Regards to Davy** - Cornell Big Red
- **Go Mules** - Central Missouri Mules
- **Growl, Bengals, Growl** - Idaho State Bengals
- **Gustie Rouser** - Gustavus Adolphus Golden Gusties
- **Hi Hi Yikas** - Appalachian State Mountaineers
- **I'm a Tar Heel Born** - North Carolina Tar Heels
- **I'm So Glad** - Tennessee State Tigers

- **On Brave Old Army Team** - Army Black Knights
- **On Saxon Warriors** - Alfred University Saxons
- **Oskee Wow Wow** - Illinois Fighting Illini
- **Peruna** - SMU Mustangs
- **Ragtime Cowboy Joe** - Wyoming Cowboys
- **Rearing Tearing** - Lehigh Mountain Hawks
- **Ride High, You Mustangs** - California Poly Mustangs
- **Ring Out, Ahoya** - Marquette Golden Eagles
- **Ring the Bells** - South Dakota State Jackrabbits
- **Sons of Westwood** - UCLA Bruins
- **Stand Up and Cheer** - Ohio University Bobcats
- **Ten Thousand Men of Harvard** - Harvard Crimson
- **Texas Fight** - Texas Longhorns
- **The Victors** - Michigan Wolverines
- **There They Go Again** - Tennessee Tech Golden Eagles
- **Tiger Rag** - Clemson Tigers
- **Tuftonia's Day** - Tufts Jumbos
- **Um Ya Ya** - St. Olaf Oles
- **Unfurl the Brown and White** - St. Bonaventure Bonnies
- **Utah Man** - Utah Utes
- **Victory is Sure** - Northwest Nazarene Crusaders
- **War Eagle** - Auburn Tigers
- **We Never Will Forget Thee** - Hamilton Continentals
- **When the Saints Go Marching In** - Providence Friars
- **Wings of Victory** - Northwest Missouri Bearcats
- **Yard By Yard** - Williams College Ephs

Dog Days: The Georgia **Bulldogs** (Athens) have been rolling with a pure white English bulldog named Uga since 1956. The name is short for the University of Georgia.

High Society: In the late 1920s, Brewton-Parker College (now Brewton-Parker Christian University) football coaches wanted something unique. In 1929, the school settled on **Barons**, a nod to nobility meant to honor the Scottish heritage of the nearby Mount Vernon community.

Kickin' It: Truett-McConnell College (Cleveland) first took the court in 1951 as the **Mountaineers**, a nod to the surrounding area. By 1966, though, it had traded the hiking boots for paws and became the **Great Danes**.

As the school added new sports, the names got quirkier – baseball was the **Diamond Danes**, and soccer was the **Kickin' Danes**. When the school transitioned to a four-year institution and rebranded as Truett-McConnell University, it settled on the **Bears** as a more representative symbol of the region.

Ramble On: The Ramblin' Wreck of Georgia Tech is a mechanical mascot that honors the school's engineering program. Today, a 1930 Ford A Model Sports Coupe in the school's colors leads the football team onto the field.

Toned Down: There is significantly less honking at board meetings after the Gainesville State **Fighting Geese** (Oakwood) were merged into the University of North Georgia, which is known as the **Nighthawks** (Dahlonega).

Hawaii

Blaze of Glory: The Chaminade University **Silverswords** (Honolulu) are named after an endangered Hawaiian plant that grows only on the slopes of Haleakalā, Mauna Kea, and Mauna Loa between 5,000 and 10,000 feet.

It's spiky, covered with silvery hairs, and survives for decades in brutal conditions. But here's the kicker: After all those years of grinding it out, once the plant finally blooms – sometimes growing up to six feet tall – it dies soon afterward.

Give A Hoot: The University of Hawaii at West Oahu **Pueo** (Kapolei) is named after a native short-eared owl species – wise, stealthy, and able to judge your study habits.

Idaho

Bird Watchers: In 1932, Northwest Nazarene College (Nampa) formed a basketball team and named it the **Preachers** because most of the players were literally studying to be just that. But that name didn't exactly strike fear into opponents, so the name eventually gave way to the **Crusaders**. That worked for decades until 2017, when the school decided the name carried too many associations with violence and religious conflicts.

The **Nighthawks** soon took flight as the new mascot. Northwest Nazarene wasn't alone, either – since 2009, at least 15 other schools across the country have also retired the **Crusaders** nickname for the same reasons.

Bodily Harm: The University of Idaho **Vandals** (Moscow) got the nickname from their 1917 basketball team's aggressive charm offensive on the court – a no autopsy no foul strategy – not from Roman history class. A sportswriter said the players vandalized their opponents while on defense, and the name stuck.

Chicken Out: Idaho State University (Pocatello) started as the Idaho Technical Institute **Bantams**, but apparently, no one wanted to cheer for chickens, so the students placed it on the chopping block. In 1921, Ralph Hutchinson became Director of Physical Education and Athletics and helped form the "I" Club, where members adopted Princeton's Bengal Tiger as their mascot. By 1931, the school paper had rebranded itself as *The Idaho Bengal*, and eventually, everyone agreed that the **Bengals** beat the birds.

Out on a Limb: In 2001, Ricks College (Rexburg) was renamed Brigham Young University–Idaho, and with the new name came a dramatic nickname shift – goodbye **Vikings**, hello trees?

The school shut down its athletics program due to budgetary reasons as it transitioned to a four-year institution, retiring a nickname that had been in use since the 1920s. In its place, administrators dusted off a speech from 1890, when principal Jacob Spori predicted the future: "The seeds we're planting today will grow and become mighty oaks and their branches will run all over the earth."

So, the school leaned into prophecy, planted four oak trees, and christened itself the BYU–Idaho **Mighty Oaks**. Their only real rivals now? Chainsaws and bark beetles.

Illinois

Book Smart: Millikin University's (Decatur) nickname didn't come from a student vote, a schoolwide contest, or even divine inspiration. Nope. In 1916, mechanical engineering professor Carl Head just declared it.

Head apparently liked two things: oversized items and blue (which students had chosen back in 1903, proving that democracy only gets you so far). So he mashed them together into **Big Blue** and slapped the nickname on posters supporting the football team. And everyone just went along with it – because when your nickname comes from a highly motivated professor, no one is stepping up to change his mind.

Can't Stay Long: Back in the early 1900s, when football was still a thing at Loyola University (Chicago), the teams were known as the **Maroon and Gold**. In 1925, the school held a contest, and the winning name was the **Grandees** – a nod to the Spanish heritage of St. Ignatius of Loyola. The only problem? No one actually liked it.

By 1926, the football team was traveling so much that writers joked the team was "rambling from state to state," and before long, they were just called the **Ramblers**. The name stuck, even after football didn't – the program ended in 1930.

Coaching Change: Before the University of Chicago even opened its doors in 1892, the Board of Trustees had already decided on goldenrod yellow as the school color. It looked great on paper. On uniforms? Not so much.

By 1894, football Coach Amos Alonzo Stagg had seen enough. The yellow ran in the wash, showed every grass stain, and, as Stagg politely put it, "had a regrettable symbolism our opponents might not be above commenting upon." Translation: Opponents were definitely calling them cowards and other unflattering names.

So Stagg and assistant J.E. Raycroft brought a bunch of maroon ribbons to a meeting. Students and faculty voted, and boom – UChicago was in the maroon business. By the end of the 1894 baseball season, the team was rocking the new shade.

The Chicago Tribune picked up on it, dropping the word **Maroons** into an article that summer. And just like that, the university was no longer buying goldenrod stuff in bulk.

Defining Moment: In 1993, Knox College (Galesburg) decided to switch its nickname to **Prairie Fire** – a nod to the school's long tradition of conducting prairie burns for more than 80 years, and because it sounds way cooler than most names.

Before that, the teams went by **Siwash**, a nickname born in 1924 from Knox graduate George Fitch's humorous short stories in *The Saturday Evening Post* about fictional "Siwash College." Fitch swore it wasn't based on Knox, but that didn't stop students from embracing "Old Siwash" anyway.

The issue? By the early 1990s, research revealed that Siwash was actually used as a derogatory term meaning "a person of unclean habits." Suddenly, the name didn't seem so charming. So Knox made the switch to **Prairie Fire** – which sounds way less like an insult and way more like a heavy metal band.

Demons Advocate: In 1907, when St. Vincent's College rebranded as DePaul University (Chicago), the teams suited up in bright red uniforms with giant Ds plastered across the chest. Not exactly a daunting look, unless your greatest fear is oversized typography.

During one early game, an announcer started referring to them as the "D-men." The name stuck – though somewhere along the way, D-men became the Demons.

But wait – it gets better. The university also had a high school attached, DePaul Academy, and they also had teams with Ds on their jerseys. To distinguish them, the university opted for red uniforms with blue Ds, while the high school wore blue uniforms with red Ds. Essentially, every game resembled a Dr. Seuss fashion experiment.

And that's how DePaul wound up with the **Blue Demons**: A nickname born from an announcer's slip, some blue letters, and a fondness for supernatural entities.

Ancient History: By the late 1940s, students at Southern Illinois University were ready for something more exciting than being called the **Maroons**. That bland label had been hanging around since the university's first teams in 1913, but in 1951, the student body finally voted to upgrade to the **Salukis**, one of the world's oldest known dog breeds, revered in ancient Egypt.

The name tied neatly into the area's regional identity as Little Egypt, a nickname rooted in an early 1800s drought that drove northern Illinois farmers southward in search of grain. It mirrored the biblical story of Joseph's brothers heading to Egypt during a famine, but no consideration was given to the "Coats of Many Colors" as a nickname.

Heart of Stone: The Moody Bible Institute **Archers** (Chicago) aren't channeling Robin Hood or medieval longbows. The nickname actually points to architecture: The school's campus features a renowned archway that students pass through on their way to class.

So when you hear **Archers**, don't picture arrows flying – envision students late for an exam, sprinting under a big stone arch. The school's mascot is Archie the Sheepdog.

Jarheads: The Western Illinois **Leathernecks** (Macomb) got their nickname straight from the Marines thanks to athletic director Ray "Rock" Hanson. In 1927, he convinced the Navy into letting the school borrow the official Marine nickname – showing that sometimes all you need to lead a team is guts, charm, and a little inter-service lobbying.

Soldier On: The Illinois College **Blueboys** (Jacksonville) is a reference to Union Army soldiers. All of the school's 1863 senior class enlisted to fight in the Civil War.

Time Change: The Greenville College **Gremlins** (Greenville) are now the Greenville University **Panthers**.

Indiana

Counting Cards: Evansville College, now the University of Evansville, was the **Pioneers** at the beginning of the 1924-25 basketball season, which was fine until they beat Louisville 59–39. The Cardinals' coach told Evansville Coach John Harmon, "You didn't have four aces up your sleeve, you had five!" Harmon repeated the line to *The Evansville Courier* sports editor Dan Scism. Both men preferred Aces over Pioneers, and Scism realized that Aces not only sounded cooler but also saved him valuable headline space. By 1926, the school added the official color to the nickname, and the **Purple Aces** were on the court.

Exercising Power: Saint Mary-of-the-Woods College proudly calls its teams the **Pomeroys**, honoring Sister Mary Joseph Pomeroy, a tireless advocate for athletics and physical fitness, because sometimes the real powerhouse on campus isn't a mascot, it's a nun in sneakers.

Good Luck: At first, the University of Notre Dame **Fighting Irish** (South Bend) used Irish Terriers as mascots – many were given the name Clashmore Mike. The school officially switched to a leprechaun mascot in 1965.

Green with Envy: The Huntington College (now Huntington University) nickname came to life in 1928 thanks to local sportswriter Cash Keller, who apparently looked at the school's basketball team in its green and scarlet uniforms and thought, "You know what this reminds me of? Robin Hood and his merry band of woodland dudes," and called them **Foresters** in the paper. The school's yearbook, *Mnemosyne*, made it official in 1931. Decades later, there have been no reports of the team stealing from the rich and giving to the poor after games.

Light It Up: In 2021, Valparaiso University retired its long-running **Crusaders** nickname. The school swapped it for **Beacons**, which reflects its motto, "In Thy Light We See Light."

Keep Quiet: At Taylor University (Upland), basketball games get weirdly festive every December. For the Silent Night game, students pack Odle Arena in full costume – everything from Santas to vikings to ducks – and then they sit there in total silence. No cheers, no chants, just a thousand people sitting soundless like it's the world's strangest Quiet Game.

Finally, when Taylor scores its 10th point, the place absolutely detonates. The silence turns into a roar, and it's basically the only time in basketball history where the crowd cares more about an early basket than the final score. It's Christmas cheer and before-finals angst combining to make a mighty cacophony as students rush the floor.

The tradition began in the late 1980s with students wearing pajamas, and in 1997, someone thought, "Hey, what if we add a creepy silence pact?" Ever since, the **Trojans** have gone 26–1 in

Silent Night games, which really makes you wonder if the other team just gets freaked out by hundreds of costumed students staring at them in total silence. To end the game, everyone sings *Silent Night,* which serves as a fitting finale.

Point in Time: The Purdue-Fort Wayne **Mastodons** (Fort Wayne) stomp onto the field in honor of a mastodon skeleton discovered at a nearby farm in 1968 – basically a prehistoric touchdown for the paleontology community.

Throw Down: In the early 1970s, Indiana University Southeast (New Albany) students voted the school's nickname to be the River Rats – gritty, local, and, maybe, accurate. Naturally, the school's naming committee vetoed it.

Then, a history professor suggested **Grenadiers**, which the task force supported. The nickname kind of fits because elite 17th-century soldiers hurling live explosives on the battlefield compares to some people's college experience. And so the River Rats were left in the sewer, while the **Grenadiers** marched into school history.

Wordplay: Students of Ball State University (Muncie) voted to change the school's nickname to **Cardinals** in 1927, replacing the **Hoosieroons** because made-up words don't pack the same punch as bright red birds.

Iowa

Blown Away: In 1895, the state of Iowa was hit by cyclones (commonly known as tornadoes today) so frequently that the weather forecast was essentially just "duck and cover."

Later that fall, Pop Warner's Iowa Agricultural College football team started the season with two rough losses, then suddenly unleashed their inner twister and flattened Northwestern 36–0. *The Chicago Tribune* summed it up perfectly with the headline: "Struck by a Cyclone." In 1898, the school rebranded to the Iowa State **Cyclones**.

Making Waves: In 2017, the University of Iowa opened the Stead Family Children's Hospital right across the street from Kinnick Stadium. From the 12th floor, kids battling illness had the perfect view of every **Hawkeye's** home game. It didn't take long for a suggestion to become a tradition.

Before the season opener against Wyoming, Iowa fan Krista Young floated an idea on Facebook: what if everyone in the stadium just turned and waved to the kids?

The post went viral, and when the first quarter ended, 69,000 fans and players stood, turned toward the hospital, and waved in support. The kids, parents, doctors, and nurses waved back. Now every home game, the entire stadium (opponents as well) pauses after the first quarter for The **Hawkeye** Wave.

Overkill: The Marycrest International University **Marauding Eagles** (Davenport) landed for the last time in 2002, with the school closing due to financial difficulties.

Proud Display: Back in the 1890s, Upper Iowa University (Fayette) decided it was time to look sharp. They sent football player W.C. Marby home for Christmas Break with a mission: Don't just bring back presents – bring back school colors.

Marby returned with ribbons in Peacock Blue and White, proving that he either had impeccable taste or got whatever was on sale. Students saw the new shade and thought, "Well, if we're going Peacock Blue, we might as well go full peacock." Thus, the flamboyant bird was adopted as the unofficial mascot. Finally, in 1919, the school paper demanded a real mascot, and by September 1920, the **Peacocks** were official.

Troubled Waters: Reivers (river bandits) started as a term for robbers and murderers in old England and Scotland. The term eventually made its way to the United States and was used to describe the thieves on the Missouri River in the 19th century.

A student vote made **Reivers** the nickname of Iowa Western (Council Bluffs) in 1972, revealing that some college kids have a soft spot for historical felons.

Kansas

Build Up: Back in 1910, Southwestern College (Winfield) students decided that being called **Preachers** or **Methodists** wasn't exactly striking fear into their opponents ("Watch out, here comes the clergy to tackle our quarterback!").

Since the school sat on a hill, ideas like Cliff-Dwellers got tossed around – but one student, Harry Hart, thought that sounded too lazy. His take: "Anybody can dwell. Builders build." People agreed, and **Moundbuilders** became the nickname because apparently, they couldn't think of anything else that builders build.

In 1927, Southwestern Dean Leroy Allen created the Moundbuilding Ceremony to cement the name. "Nobody but **Moundbuilders** can build mounds. So, no other college has now or ever is likely to have such a custom." And he was right.

Now, every year, students pile rocks into a giant mound to prove once again that Southwestern may not have chosen the fiercest nickname, but at least they have follow-through.

God of Thunder: Only one school has a cheer that implores the god Thor to drive his thunderbolts into the opposing team. In Swedish, fans yell Rockar! Stockar! at games for the Bethany College **Swedes** (Lindsborg), asking that the opposing squad be zapped. Swedish immigrants founded the town and the school in the late 1880s. The football team was so intimidating in the early 1900s that it was known as the **Terrible Swedes**.

***Reap the Harvest*:** The nickname **Wheat Shockers** first appeared in 1904 on a poster promoting a Fairmount College football game against the Chilocco Indians. The team manager coined it since many players spent their off-seasons harvesting, or "shocking" wheat. Instead of something fierce like **Tigers** or **Warriors**, Fairmount went with a name equally terrifying to opponents: The prospect of hard manual labor. Over time, the "Wheat" was dropped, and in 1964, the school officially became the Wichita State **Shockers**.

Rock Out: The Bethel College **Threshers** (North Newton) are named after a wheat harvesting device known as the threshing stone, which was used by Russian Mennonite settlers, who moved to Kansas in the early 1870s.

Kentucky

***Bird Watchers*:** The University of Louisville proudly calls itself the **Cardinals** and favors anything red and black, but no one actually knows why. Legend pins the credit on Ellen Patterson, wife of the Arts and Sciences dean, who supposedly offered the name and official colors in 1913 at a board meeting. The only issue? The *Louisville Courier-Journal* was already referring to the Louisville teams as the **Cardinals** in 1912 and had referred to the football team as the **Red and Black** the same year. No little bird has stopped by and cleared up the confusion yet.

Chunky: Big Red, the unmistakable mascot of the Western Kentucky University **Hilltoppers** (Bowling Green), is basically a giant red blob with attitude. Created by a student in 1979 to capture the "spirit of Western," Big Red has strutted onto ESPN commercials and even adorned football helmets. Who knew a shapeless crimson blob could become a legend?

Play the Horses: Murray State's (Murray) first athletic nickname was the **Thoroughbreds**, a nod to Kentucky's horse industry. But the mouthful proved tricky for headline writers, who quickly trimmed it down to T-Breds, 'Breds, Race Horses, and Racers. By the late 1950s, **Racers** became the official moniker across campus, well, almost. Murray State baseball stubbornly held onto the **'Breds** until 2014, when they finally joined the rest of the stable.

Pray Tell: In 1917, Centre College (Danville) added a word to adjust its nickname to the **Praying Colonels** after fullback Bob Mathias led the team in prayer for teammate Bo McMillin's family before a game against Kentucky. McMillin, who had never kicked in a game before that day, booted the game-winning field goal for a 3-0 victory.

Four years later, Centre pulled off the biggest upset in college football to that point, defeating Harvard 6-0 and ending its five-year winning streak. That season, the **Praying Colonels** went undefeated at 10-0, surrendering only a single touchdown. Today, the school is known as the **Colonels**.

Louisiana

Cajun Spice: The Southwestern Louisiana Institute once went by the **Bulldogs**, but in the early 1960s, the school leaned into its French roots and became the University of the Southwestern Louisiana **Raging Cajuns**.

A couple of years later, somebody decided that the last "g" was just too uptight, so it got swapped for an apostrophe – hello **Ragin' Cajuns**. In 1999, the school changed its name to the University of Louisiana at Lafayette. Since 2017, the Sun Belt Conference has referred to them simply as Louisiana.

Change of Heart: Tulane University (New Orleans) is the **Green Wave** – a nickname inspired by the song *The Rolling Green Wave* which was written in support of the then **Greenback** football team. By 1920, students and newspapers decided it was easier to ride a wave than just sing about one.

Cool Cats: Southern University (Baton Rouge) started as the **Bushmen**, then moved to **Cats**, then got a little more specific with **Jaguar Cats**, before finally deciding to go with just **Jaguars**.

Formality: The nicknames for the women's and men's athletics teams at Centenary College of Louisiana (Shreveport) are the **Ladies** and the **Gentlemen**. Some bouncers near campus might not always agree with those monikers.

Marching Orders: LSU Alexandria went with the clear choice for a nickname – **Generals**. Central Louisiana was host to the 1941 Louisiana Maneuvers, which brought 350,000 troops to the area in preparation for World War II. Among them were Omar Bradley, Dwight D. Eisenhower, and George Patton.

Real Deal: Louisiana State University (Baton Rouge) has the only live tiger mascot in the country. The first tiger was bought from the Little Rock Zoo for $750 in 1936 and named after athletic trainer Mike Chambers. Since then, seven Mikes (all Bengals or Bengal mixes) have carried the title. Starting in 2017, it was announced that Mike would no longer leave his on-campus habitat to attend games, sadly missing out on some legendary tailgate parties.

Vote of Confidence: In 1923, Northwestern State University (Natchitoches) held a school-wide election to pick a nickname from student nominations. The winner? **Demons** – earning the submitter $10. It defeated Sharks, Daredevils, Musketeers, Pelicans, Prather's Ground Hogs, Bloodhounds, Serpents, and Cyclops (because apparently one-eyed monsters don't have the best perspective on college sports).

Mascot Names

- **Action C** - Central Michigan Chippewas (letter C)
- **Albert and Alberta Gator** - Florida Gators
- **Archibald McGrowl** - Misericordia Cougars
- **Aristocat** - Tennessee State Tigers
- **Avalanche** - Kutztown Golden Bears
- **Baldwin & Gladys** - Mary Baldwin Fighting Squirrels
- **Bananas T. Bear** - Maine Black Bears
- **Bevo** - Texas Longhorns (live steer)
- **Big Al** - Alabama Crimson Tide (elephant)
- **Blizzard T. Husky** - Michigan Tech Huskies
- **Brown Dawg & Grey Dawg** - Southern Illinois Salukis
- **Buzz** - Georgia Tech Yellow Jackets
- **Chompers** - Allegheny Gators
- **Cutlass T. Crusader** - Clarke Pride
- **Dunker** - Murray State Racers
- **Finn** - Landmark Sharks
- **Freedom** - Georgia Southern Eagles (live eagle)
- **Gaylord & Gladys** - Campbell Fighting Camels
- **Gnarls** - The New School Narwhals
- **Gunrock** - UC Davis Aggies (mustang)
- **Handsome Dan** - Yale Bulldogs (live bulldog)
- **Kaboom** - Bradley Braves (gargoyle)
- **Kid and Play** - Texas Southern Tigers
- **LaCumba** - Southern Jaguars

- **LeeRoy** - Trinity Tigers
- **Magnus** - Cleveland State Vikings
- **Mingus** - Berklee College of Music (cat)
- **Paws** - Northeastern Huskies
- **Paydirt Pete** - UTEP Miners
- **PeeDee** - East Carolina Pirates
- **Pegasus** - Central Florida Knights (live horse)
- **Porky** - Texas A&M Kingsville Javelinas
- **R.B. Bbhoggawact** - Austin CC Riverbats
- **Reveille** - Texas A&M (live Border Collie)
- **Shel** - Florida Keys Tortugas
- **Stella** - Temple Owls (live owl)
- **Stevie Pointer** - Wisconsin-Stevens Point Pointers
- **Stomper** - Minnesota State Mavericks
- **Sturgis** - Kennesaw State Owls (live owl)
- **Testudo** - Maryland Terrapins
- **Texan Rider** - Tarleton State Texans
- **Tim the Beaver** - MIT Engineers
- **Timeout** - Fresno State Bulldogs
- **True Grit** - UMBC Retrievers
- **Uga** - Georgia Bulldogs (live bulldog)
- **Venom** - Florida A&M Rattlers
- **Yank** - Hampden-Sydney Tigers
- **Yosef** - Appalachian State Mountaineers
- **Zippy** - Akron Zips (kangaroo)

Maine

Bear Witness: Bowdoin College (Brunswick) went Arctic in 1913 when Professor Frank Whittier suggested the **Polar Bears** as the school nickname. The frosty pick honored alumnus Robert Peary (Class of 1877), who became the first man to reach the North Pole in 1909, with fellow Bowdoin grad Donald MacMillan (Class of 1898) by his side. Two years later, MacMillan gifted Bowdoin a mounted polar bear, which still greets visitors in Morrell Gym as Bowdoin's longest-standing athlete.

Headstrong: Colby College (Waterville) went without a nickname or mascot until 1923, when the school paper's editor suggested the football team trade in its "dark horse" status for something more memorable – a white mule. Before long, students were borrowing actual farm mules to cheer from the sidelines, and the **Mules** became the nickname. These days, it's a little less hay, with a student donning the Morty the Mule costume at games.

Irritant: The College of the Atlantic **Black Flies** (Bar Harbor) honors the dreaded nuisance that ruins outdoor summer activities.

Poke the Bear: The University of Maine's mascot history is as wild as a frat party in 1910s Bangor. First, there were stories of students swiping a live elephant (and later a giant tin elephant sign) because, apparently, early Maine mascot traditions involved casual grand theft pachyderm.

Things got less criminal – but furrier – in 1912, when a retired police chief loaned the school a black bear cub named Jeff, who debuted at a football game against Colby. The following year, Maine tried to mix it up with a moose named Napoleon. Spoiler: Nobody liked the moose.

By 1914, Jeff was back, and the crowd went bananas – literally. The bear was renamed "Bananas," and the **Black Bears** nickname was made official. Because let's face it, the Maine Elephants doesn't sound right.

Maryland

Goat Luck: The U.S. Naval Academy (Annapolis) kicked off its mascot tradition with a pet goat named El Cid, brought to the 1893 Army–Navy game by sailors from the cruiser New York. The goat brought good luck – the **Midshipmen** won 6–3. Since the early 1900s, Bill the Goat and his successors have roamed the Navy sidelines, probably judging everyone's snacks.

Green with Mystery: No one can quite agree on how McDaniel College (Westminster) ended up as the **Green Terror**. One tale claims a writer called the football team the "green terrors" due to their uniforms and tackling abilities. Another says Coach D.K. Shroyer boosted morale after a loss by calling his squad "a bunch of terrors." The only thing everyone agrees on? Record-keeping in the 1920s was about as sturdy as a paper playbook in a rainstorm.

Sailing Away: The Chesapeake College **Skipjacks** (Wye Mills) nickname refers to the sailboats used on the shallow waters of Chesapeake Bay for hauling oysters.

Shell Game: The University of Maryland (College Park) used to go by the **Old Liners** – a nod to the state's nickname – but nobody was exactly lining up to cheer for that. In 1932, the school newspaper sought something fresher. Enter football Coach Dr. H. Curley Byrd, who pitched the **Terrapins**, inspired by the Chesapeake Bay turtles beloved in his hometown of Crisfield. The name stuck, and soon Maryland had a hard-shelled new identity.

Massachusetts

Adjudicators: Brandeis University (Waltham) has been the **Judges** since its 1948 founding, honoring Louis D. Brandeis, the first Jewish Supreme Court Justice. It does not have a law school.

Big Deal: Amherst College takes its name from Amherst, Massachusetts, itself named after 18th-century British General Jeffery Amherst. For decades, the school's teams were informally known as the **Lord Jeffs** – until 2016, when trustees voted to retire the nickname after acknowledging the general's suggestion to use smallpox-infected blankets against Native Americans during the French and Indian War.

A campus-wide vote crowned the **Mammoths** as the new mascot, inspired by the Columbian Mammoth skeleton in the school's

Museum of Natural History. The extinct giant trampled the competition, beating out options like the Hamsters (an anagram of Amherst) and the Poets (a nod to Emily Dickinson, who studied at Amherst Academy).

Changing Ways: Springfield College has strutted through a colorful collection of nicknames – **Stubby Christians**, **Gymnasts**, **Maroons**, and **Chiefs** – before settling on the majestic **Pride**, giving the school a roar that's more regal.

Puppy Love: In 1922, Boston University students had intense debates leading up to a mascot showdown: Bull Moose vs. Boston Terrier. The moose had size, the dog had heart. Students went with the **Terriers** – partly because the breed was born in 1869, the same year BU was chartered, and partly because no one wanted to clean up after a moose.

Years later, after *Gone with the Wind* became a best-seller, the mascot terrier got his name: Rhett. Why Rhett? Because Rhett loved Scarlett – and BU's official color is Scarlet. Which means this may be the only case in mascot history where a dog was named after a fictional guy just to make a color pun.

Revolutionary: The Massachusetts Agricultural College **Aggies** farmed out wins until 1948, when the school rebranded as the University of Massachusetts Amherst **Redmen**. That name lasted until 1972, when a group of Native Americans pointed out that maybe using that as a nickname wasn't the best idea. UMass scrambled for a replacement, and the Student Senate landed on the **Minutemen** – the colonial militia from the Revolutionary War who were ready to fight at a moment's notice. The first Minutemen organized in Massachusetts in 1774.

Michigan

Beastly Nature: The Gogebic Community College **Samsons** (Ironwood) are said by the school to honor mythical creatures that roam the dense woods of Michigan's Upper Peninsula.

Charge It: By the late 1960s, Hillsdale College decided its long-time nickname**, Dales**, wasn't getting the job done anymore. The school eventually narrowed down a gargantuan list of more than 900 replacement names to one: **Chargers**. Students approved in a landslide vote, and the new identity was born in 1968. Football Coach Frank "Muddy" Waters backed the change, too, shrugging, "After all, what's a **Dale**?"

Great Scot: In 1931, Alma College retired the **Fighting Presbyterians** nickname and became the **Scots**. The town of Alma proudly calls itself "Scotland, U.S.A.," and the college leans all the way in, including hosting an annual Highland Festival. The marching band wears kilts. And so does the head football coach, who wears one at home games – creating a unique home-field advantage where opposing players all have the lingering question, "Wait … what's he wearing under there?"

Name Drop: When Michigan Agricultural College rebranded as Michigan State in 1925, they figured it was time to ditch the **Aggies** nickname as well.

A school group reviewed the hundreds of suggestions and picked the **Staters**. Because apparently, creativity hadn't been invented yet or the other nominees were amazingly terrible.

Local sports editor George Alderton hated the name so much he refused to use it in print and vowed to find a better one. Depending on the version, Alderton solved the nickname dilemma by either digging up **Spartans** from the scrap pile of rejected names the committee had already reviewed or having it handed to him by Greek immigrant and coffee shop owner George Scofes, who suggested the **Spartans** and explained who they were.

Alderton soon after put it in the paper without giving the school a heads up or thanking Scofes, and it stuck. So Michigan State's nickname is the result of journalistic pettiness and some dumb luck, or a Greek guy who knew his history.

Naming Names: Albion College didn't overthink it when picking a nickname – it went with **Britons**, the Celtic people who lived in Great Britain during the Iron Age until the Romans arrived. Since the Britons were among the first to settle Great Britain, the college tipped its hat to one of the island's oldest names: Albion.

Space Race: Before 1932, Olivet College (now the University of Olivet) went by the **Congregationalists** – a nickname that looked awkward on paper and took half the game just to shout from the stands. A student vote championed the **Comets**, beating out the Reds, Pioneers, Vets, and Falcons. Then, in true Olivet fashion, someone added Crimson after the fact because apparently one word didn't have enough syllables to their liking. The **Crimson Comets** streaked across campus for just a single year before fading away and reverting to just **Comets**.

Tunnel Vision: Nazareth College (Kalamazoo) closed in 1992, taking the nickname **Moles** with it.

Minnesota

Keeping Busy: In 1932, Bemidji State University President Manfred Deputy watched football practice and declared the players were "working like beavers." That was enough for him to huddle up with the team and announce, "I christen this team the **Beavers**." No vote, no committee, just one guy blurting out the first hardworking animal that came to mind. The school is lucky that President Deputy wasn't a donkey enthusiast.

Off the Rails: The University of Minnesota's (Minneapolis) nickname boils down to two things: Political satire and tricking people with fashion choices. In 1857, a political cartoonist mocked legislators for pushing through a $5 million railroad bonding bill by drawing them as gophers with human heads pulling a cart of bondholders. The bill passed, but people remembered the rodents, and soon the Gopher State nickname stuck.

Fast forward to the 1920s, when the University of Minnesota adopted the **Gophers** as its nickname. In 1934, Coach Bernie Bierman put his team in all-gold uniforms so the football would blend in, confusing defenses, or so he hoped, causing broadcaster Halsey Hall to start calling them the **Golden Gophers**.

Bon Voyage: The Minnesota North College – Rainy River **Voyageurs** (International Falls) nickname matches the name of nearby Voyageurs National Park. Both honor the French-Canadian fur traders who were the first non-natives to the area.

Pipe Dreams: Hamline University (St. Paul) took its name from founder Bishop Leonidas Lent Hamline, making the choice of a nickname surprisingly simple. Inspired by the German folklore story, the Pied Piper of Hamelin, Germany, famously lured rats – and later children – out of town with his music.

The **Pipers** were an obvious choice because when your mascot's résumé includes pest control and child abduction, the intimidation factor is way off the charts.

Mississippi

A Good Egg: In 1927, students from Mississippi and Mississippi State created the Golden Egg Trophy to crown the winner of their annual rivalry game. Fast forward to 1979: Both teams were so bad they couldn't even sniff a postseason bowl game. *The Clarion-Ledger* sports editor Tom Patterson figured if they couldn't play in a real bowl, they could at least play in an Egg Bowl. And it's been called that ever since.

Mail Ballot: The University of Mississippi **Rebels** (Oxford) was one of five proposed nicknames sent to writers for their input in 1936. Almost all the respondents identified the Rebels as their preferred name. An earlier contest in 1929 had named Mississippi Flood as the winner, but that nickname never caught on.

More Cowbell: Legend has it that about 70 years ago, during a heated Mississippi State-Ole Miss game, a cow wandered onto the field. The **Bulldogs** went on to win, and suddenly the cow was less "random cattle" and more "divine bovine."

Lugging good luck livestock around got old fast, so fans swapped the animal for its accessory of choice – the cowbell.

During games, bells rang so loud and for so long that in 1974, the Southeastern Conference banned fans from using all artificial noisemakers. A later compromise allowed cowbells to be rung only until the offense gets into formation, a rule Mississippi State fans follow, creatively, especially if it's a crucial third down play in the fourth quarter.

Missouri

Pack Pride: Back in 1919, the State Normal School for the Second Normal District (which must have looked awesome on jerseys) rebranded as the Central Missouri State Teachers College (Warrensburg). Students didn't want to be called the **Normals** or the **Teachers** anymore, so in 1922, the school launched a naming contest (things moved slowly back then). Suggestions came pouring in – Hippopotamuses, Bobcats, and Skunks were nominated. (Smell That Touchdown!)

The winning pick? **Mules**. Missouri had a reputation for breeding some of the finest mules in the country, and the name carried both grit and state pride. Fast forward to 1974, when the women's teams got their own nickname: **Jennies** (female donkeys).

Jump Ahead: Back in 1936, Kansas City University (today University of Missouri-Kansas City) didn't have athletic teams. So the school newspaper staff figured the debate team deserved a catchy nickname. Their inspiration quite literally hopped into town when the Kansas City Zoo bought two baby kangaroos. Some students loved the idea of the **Kangaroos**; others thought it was silly. The name was up in the air – until Walt Disney himself weighed in. Disney sketched a kangaroo alongside Mickey Mouse for the cover of the school's humor magazine, and suddenly the Roo had a celebrity endorsement. Eventually, the nickname became official – proving that if Goofy's boss says you're a Kangaroo, then you're a Kangaroo.

Sea Change: For more than 40 years, the University of Missouri–St. Louis went by the **Rivermen**. However, by 2007, students were no longer thrilled with the nickname. Let's just say **Riverwomen** wasn't inspiring anybody. So the school ditched the nickname for **Tritons** – technically newts (the salamander kind) named after the Greek god of the sea. And so far, everyone is cool with being mythological salamanders.

Street Smarts: The Webster University **Gorloks** (St. Louis) nickname was created in 1984 by combining the names of Gore Avenue and Lockwood Avenue, which intersected in the heart of "Old Webster." A Gorlok is now listed as a mythical creature combining traits of a cheetah, buffalo, and St. Bernard – something that probably made more sense at 3 a.m. after consuming too many adult beverages.

Montana

Night to Remember: Montana State–Northern (Havre) calls its men's and women's teams the **Northern Lights** and **Skylights**, capturing the celestial beauty of the region – and making it perfectly clear that their opponents should feel dim in comparison.

Otter Nonsense: When Great Falls College went hunting for its first nickname, students nominated more than 100 names in 2023. After some early voting and a heated runoff, the **River Otters** swam away with the win, narrowly edging out the Electric Elk (which sounds like an incredible rock band or a rare Pokémon). The Wolverines finished a distant third.

Prepare for Battle: After Intermountain Union College and Billings Polytechnic Institute merged, Coach Herb Klindt pushed for a contest to name the new school. Rocky Mountain College came out on top, and Klindt himself got to give it a nickname – the **Bears**. That lasted until 1983, when a vote added a little more grit and turned them into the **Battlin' Bears** because apparently, alliterative bears are scarier than the regular ones.

Nebraska

Batter Up: The University of Nebraska (Lincoln) went through a zoo of early nicknames – **Nebraskans**, **Old Gold Knights**, **Antelopes**, **Tree Planters**, **Rattlesnake Boys**, and the infamous **Bugeaters**. Apparently, the sight of bull bats devouring insects across the plains inspired the last one.

Sportswriter Charles Sherman decided eating bugs didn't sound dignified, so in 1900, he borrowed **Cornhuskers** from the University of Iowa (who had tossed the nickname aside) and made it stick by using it in his articles – saving Nebraska from a lifetime of entomological confusion.

Graceful: The Nebraska-Kearney **Lopers** is one of two U.S. schools to abbreviate antelope in their nickname.

Nevada

Pack Mentality: The University of Nevada's (Reno) first athletic teams were known as the **Sagebrushers**, **Sage Hens**, or **Sage Warriors** – all names with a distinctly botanical theme. Then, in 1921, a sportswriter observed the Nevada defense tearing it up and described them as looking like "a pack of wolves."

The nickname stuck, becoming official in 1923 as the **Wolves**, and then upgraded to the **Wolf Pack** in 1928. Because one wolf is cool, but a whole pack? Much more fun.

Rebel Yell: Why is the University of Nevada, Las Vegas (UNLV) known as the **Rebels**? It depends on who you ask. The official line is that the nickname came in the mid-1950s during a wave of cultural rebellion – think *Rebel Without a Cause*, early rock 'n' roll, and Elvis swiveling his hips on TV.

The school insists it is not Civil War-related, but for a few decades, the mascot did dress in a Confederate soldier uniform. Others say the name was a jab at its bigger, older, and better-funded rival up north at the University of Nevada (Reno) – a way of saying, "We don't play by your rules and pretty soon we're going to be so good at basketball they're going to call us the **Runnin' Rebels**."

That'll Sting: The Nevada State University **Scorpions** (Henderson) are the only school in the nation with that nickname.

New Hampshire

Drink Up: Dartmouth (Hanover) students decided that the **Big Green** nickname does not lend itself to a mascot, which is why they created Keggy the Keg, an anthropomorphic beer dispenser, to show up at campus functions.

Writing in Ink: Southern New Hampshire University (Manchester) started as the New Hampshire School of Accounting and Commerce in 1933. Its nickname, **Penmen**, honors the people who used pens and needed good penmanship to get the job done – accountants, clerks, and other business trades.

New Jersey

Give a Damn: Rutgers University (New Brunswick) is a big fan of scarlet. The school is the **Scarlet Knights**, while Rutgers-Newark is the **Scarlet Raiders** and Rutgers-Camden is the **Scarlet Raptors**. It's not a color – it's a lifestyle.

Knight School: New Jersey City University takes its nickname from architecture. Hepburn Hall, a Collegiate Gothic-style building, inspired the school's nickname, the **Gothic Knights**. The structure, completed in 1930 on the school's campus, was designed by the Guilbert and Betelle architecture firm.

Pine Power: In the late 1980s, students at Rowan College at Burlington County (Mount Laurel) needed a nickname and went with the **Barons** – a nod to the New Jersey Pine Barrens nearby.

Forget castles and noblemen – in South Jersey, being a **Baron** means you rule over pine trees, cranberry bogs, and maybe the Jersey Devil if he shows up.

Salad Days: Felician University (Lodi and Rutherford) was almost a bunch of vegetables. When the school launched its athletic department in the mid-1990s, a naming contest came down to two finalists: Falcons and Tomatoes. Director of Athletics Bob Symons went with the Falcons, then added a colorful descriptor to create the **Golden Falcons**. Probably a good call – because if you're the tomatoes, then you never catch up.

Teaching Lesson: The Rowan University **Profs** (Glassboro) nickname celebrates the school's past as a teachers' college, dating back to when it was known as the Glassboro Normal School.

New Mexico

Hungry Like the Wolf: On Oct.1, 1920, the University of New Mexico (Albuquerque) student newspaper rolled out the **Lobos** (Spanish for wolves) as the school's new nickname and mascot by proclaiming, "The Lobo is respected for his cunning, feared for his prowess, and is the leader of the pack. It is the ideal name for the Varsity boys who go forth to battle for the glory of the school. All together now; fifteen rahs for the LOBOS." And then most likely, exhausted students collapsed all over the campus from cheer fatigue, trying to accomplish the suggested 15 yells.

Loners: The Luna Community College **Rough Riders** (Las Vegas) and the Mesaland Community **Stampede** (Tucumcari, NM) are the only schools with those nicknames. No other schools dare to saddle up to them.

New York

Bray Day: The United States Military Academy (West Point) has mules as mascots because an officer at the Philadelphia Quartermaster Depot decided that Army needed something to counter Navy. The **Midshipmen** had brought a goat to the Army-Navy game starting in 1890. Army responded – albeit a little late – with an ice-wagon mule adorned with streamers and a gray blanket for the 1899 game. Army won 17-5. There are currently three animals in the Mule Corps, which also serve as the mascots for the U.S. Army.

Burning Bridges: Brooklyn College started as the **Kingsmen** but switched to **Bridges** in 1994 – probably hoping to connect with something more concrete. By 2010, the school decided to bulldoze the metaphor and go with the **Bulldogs**.

Code Red: In 1905, Cornell (Ithaca) had no nickname, so recent grad Romeyn Berry wrote "big red team" into a football song lyric. The phrase stuck, and Berry was rewarded with the princely sum of $25, which, even adjusted for inflation, is a pretty lousy payout for inventing a century-long brand. Go **Big Red**!

Fully Charged: In 2023, Union College (Schenectady) pulled the plug on **Dutchmen** and **Dutchwomen** and rebranded as the **Garnet Chargers**. Garnet has been the school color for more than 150 years, and Chargers is a nod to the area's history of electrical innovation – Thomas Edison moved his Edison Machine Works there in 1887 – because nothing fires up school spirit quite like honoring the 19th-century industrial relocation.

It Bears Watching: Until 1961, Potsdam State (now SUNY Potsdam) was known as the **Racquetteers**, a nickname that was both difficult to spell and oddly specific. So, students held multiple naming contests and ultimately settled on **Polar Bears**, and a pink-and-white costume was eventually found. Students hated it. By 1964, they'd rebelled once more, trimmed the name down to just **Bears**, and purchased a much fiercer costume. Lesson learned: From **Racquetteers** to **Polar Bears** to **Bears** – sometimes the rebrand is about thinking in fewer letters (and less pink fur).

Name Drop Bomb: In 1938, Ithaca College students voted overwhelmingly for **Cayugas** as their athletic teams' nickname, referencing the Native American tribe from central New York. Problem solved, right? Not quite. Within a few years, the teams mysteriously started to become the **Bombers**. Nobody's really sure why. Some say a sportswriter just preferred it and kept typing it until it stuck. Others point to the early-1940s bomber craze – the Air Force, the Bronx Bombers, Joe Louis was known as the "Brown Bomber," and Ithaca just wanted to be like the cool kids.

Off Color: Syracuse University originally chose rose pink and pea green as its official colors in 1872, which left its uniforms resembling a poor wallpaper choice. The school tried again with rose tint and azure, then pink and blue, which probably left many demanding to know who is in charge of making these decisions.

In 1889, after a football win over Hamilton College, everyone was still too busy mocking their color scheme to talk about the game. So a committee was formed to select something that would not cause opposing fans to point and giggle. After trying out different combinations someone had an idea: "Hey, nobody else is using orange." By 1890, orange became the official color. Teams were called the Orangemen, the Orangewomen were added in 1971, and finally, in 2004, they simplified all of it to the **Orange**.

On Tap: Vassar College (Poughkeepsie) didn't have to ferment too many ideas for a nickname. The **Brewers** honor the school's founder, Matthew Vassar, who launched his business empire by opening a brewery at 19. Cheers to higher learning!

Royal Treatment: Columbia University (New York) adopted the **Lions** as its nickname in 1910 when the Student Board unveiled a banner featuring *Leo Columbiae* (Lion of Columbia). Former student George Brokow had suggested the lion as a nod to the school's royal roots – Columbia was originally King's College, chartered in 1754 by King George II.

Additionally, lions are featured on the English coat of arms, making it all fit nicely. Basically, Columbia wanted to remind everyone that "We're not just any college – we're royalty."

Stretch Out: The Manhattan College **Jaspers** (Bronx) is an honorific for Brother Jasper of Mary, who arrived in 1861 and essentially invented extracurricular activities on campus. He started clubs, bands, became the first athletic director, and even brought baseball to the school.

Manhattan swears he also gave the world the 7th inning stretch, because he would pause the games and insist that student spectators get up and move around after sitting for seven innings. Supposedly, when Manhattan played exhibition games against the New York Giants at the Polo Grounds in the 1890s, the habit spread, eventually allowing the Houston Astros to play *Deep in the Heart of Texas* at every home game.

Top Chefs: The Culinary Institute of America **Steels** (Hyde Park) are named after the tool used to sharpen knives.

North Carolina

Battering: The University of North Carolina **Tar Heels** (Chapel Hill) have had a ram as their mascot since 1924, when head cheerleader Vic Huggins came up with the idea to honor former

Tar Heel fullback Jack Merritt, who was known as "the battering ram." Rameses the First made its debut at a game against the Virginia Military Institute, where the North Carolina kicker rubbed the ram's horns for good luck before making a late 30-yard field goal to give the **Tar Heels** a 3-0 win.

Holy Smokes: North Carolina Wesleyan University (Rocky Mount) is home to the **Battling Bishops**, a name that, according to the school, dates back to the concept of traveling missionaries in Europe who would sometimes participate in military campaigns. Picture it: Riding through the countryside with little more than a Bible, a few belongings, a willingness to preach, and throw some punches if necessary.

Horn to Be Wild: Gaston College (Dallas) could never settle on a nickname. First they were the **Raiders**, then the **Rebels**, then the **Warriors**, before scrapping athletics entirely in the early 1970s. Decades later, when sports made a comeback, they skipped all the recycled mascot options and went with **Rhinos**, the only school with that nickname in the country.

OK Boomer: In 1932, Western Carolina football Coach C.C. Poindexter held a contest to pick the school's new nickname. The finalists? Catamounts (wildcats) and Mountain Boomers (ground squirrels, not stiff drinks from a still). The **Catamounts** won, which is fine and all, but think of what we all could have had.

Print the Legend: Campbell University (Buies Creek) swears its **Fighting Camels** nickname comes from a heroic pep talk in 1900. After a fire destroyed the school, then known as Buies Creek Academy, founder J.A. Campbell was ready to throw in the towel until his neighbor, Zachary Kivett, told him to quit sulking: "Jim Archie, why are you in bed? I thought Campbells had a hump on them." Inspiring, right? Except the school actually went by the **Hornets** until January 1934, when someone randomly swapped in **Camels**. Why? No one really knows. Maybe it was a nod to Camel cigarettes, perhaps it was because a student doodled camels on banquet name cards, or maybe they just realized Campbell **Camels** sounded way cooler than Campbell **Hornets**.

Punch It: Back in the 1920s, Elon College teams were known as the **Fightin' Christians**. In 2000, the school decided it was time for a rebirth – literally – and became the **Phoenix**, rising from the ashes of its old nickname with considerably less knockouts.

Wind of Change: Catawba College (named after the county it was founded in) adopted the nickname **Indians** in 1927. In 2005, the NCAA began enforcing rules against nicknames and imagery considered hostile or abusive to Native Americans. Soon after, Catawba College entered discussions with leaders of the Catawba Indian Nation regarding the use of the name.

In 2006, the NCAA exempted the school, allowing it to use the nickname **Catawba Indians** (never just Indians) with the support of the Catawba Indian Nation – creating the Catawba College **Catawba Indians** (Salisbury).

Wolf Gang: In 1921, a few years after becoming North Carolina State College, the school began searching for a new athletic nickname. According to legend, the administration received a letter from an anonymous alumnus: in one version, they suggested "Wolf Pack" because it sounded tough; in another, they complained that the football players were behaving like an unruly pack of wolves.

Either way, the football program adopted **Wolfpack**, while the school's other teams continued to use earlier nicknames like **Aggies**, **Farmers**, or **Techs**.

In 1925, new red uniforms and the strong play of team captain Rochelle "Red" Johnson inspired the basketball team's nickname of the **Red Terrors**.

In 1946, with U.S. veterans on campus through the GI Bill, some questioned whether **Wolfpack** should remain, since Adolf Hitler had also used the term for German U-boat groups during World War II. A slate of alternatives was considered, including the North Staters, Cardinals, Hornets, Cultivators, Cotton Pickers, Pine-rooters (pigs), Auctioneers, and Calumets. None of these gained traction, and **Wolfpack** endured, eventually being adopted by the school and all North Carolina State athletic teams.

One & Only

- Washtenaw CC **Alphas** (Ann Arbor, MI)
- Ursuline **Arrows** (Pepper Pike, OH)
- Clatsop CC **Bandits** (Astoria, OR)
- Presbyterian **Blue Hose** (Clinton, SC)
- Florida State College **BlueWaves** (Jacksonville, FL)
- Wisconsin-Eau Claire **Blugolds** (WI)
- Clovis CC **Crush** (Fresno, CA)
- Loras College **Duhawks** (Dubuque, IA)
- Mary Baldwin **Fighting Squirrels** (Staunton, VA)
- Panola **Fillies** (Carthage, TX)
- Arizona Christian **Firestorm** (Phoenix, AZ)
- Wayland Baptist **Flying Queens** (Plainview, TX)
- Haverford College **Fords** (PA)
- Swarthmore College **Garnet** (PA)
- Xavier **Gold Nuggets** (New Orleans, LA)
- NE Oklahoma A&M **Golden Norsemen** (Miami, OK)
- Jackson State CC **Green Jays** (TN)
- Texas A&M-Corpus Christi **Islanders** (TX)
- Brookdale CC **Jersey Blues** (Lincroft, NJ)
- Erie CC **Kats** (Williamsville, NY)
- Columbia College **Koalas** (SC)
- Hesston **Larks** (KS)
- Lasell **Lasers** (Newton, MA)
- Onondaga CC **Lazers** (Syracuse, NY)

- Tennessee-Chattanooga **Mocs** (TN)
- Bismarck **Mystics** (ND)
- Washington & Jefferson **Presidents** (PA)
- Angelo State **Rambelles** (San Angelo, TX)
- Austin CC **Riverbats** (TX)
- Texas A&M-Galveston **Sea Aggies** (TX)
- Pace University **Setters** (New York, NY)
- Saint Mary **Spires** (Leavenworth, KS)
- Salem College **Spirits** (Winston-Salem, NC)
- Texas College **Steers** (Tyler, TX)
- Fresno Pacific **Sunbirds** (CA)
- Central New Mexico **Suncats** (Albuquerque, NM)
- Cincinnati State **Surge** (OH)
- Williston State **Tetons** (ND)
- Dallas-Richland **Thunderducks** (Dallas, TX)
- San Diego **Toreros** (CA)
- Ohio-Zanesville **Tracers** (OH)
- McDowell Tech **Trekkers** (Marion, NC)
- Monroe CC **Tribunes** (Rochester, NY)
- Columbia-Greene CC **Twins** (Hudson, NY)
- Logan College **Vols** (Carterville, IL)
- Kingsborough CC **Wave** (Brooklyn, NY)
- Galveston College **Whitecaps** (TX)
- Randolph **WildCats** (Lynchburg, VA)
- Cleveland CC **Yetis** (NC)

not all single use nicknames are listed

North Dakota

Blue Note: In 1974, Dickinson State University decided it was time to say goodbye to its earlier nicknames – the **Normal Lights** and the **Savages** – and went with something more enduring. It landed on the **Blue Hawks**, a combination of the school's official color and the indigenous sparrow hawk.

Come Out Fighting: In 1930, the University of North Dakota (Grand Forks) adopted the nickname **Fighting Sioux** after a student suggested it to counter rival North Dakota State's choice of the Bison. By 2012, the NCAA ruled the name "hostile and abusive," and that same year, state residents voted to replace it.

Without support from the state's two Sioux tribes, the name and logo were officially retired in 2015. A student and alums vote followed, and **Fighting Hawks** soared past the other finalists – North Stars, Nodaks, Roughriders, and Sundogs – to become the new identity.

Ohio

All for One: In 1925, Xavier University (Cincinnati) adopted the **Musketeers** as its nickname after board member Rev. Francis J. Finn pitched it as the perfect fit, inspired by the character D'Artagnan from Alexandre Dumas' *The Three Musketeers*. He also liked that the book tied into Xavier's French heritage and captured the whole "all for one, one for all" thing.

Fun fact: D'Artagnan wasn't one of the three Musketeers from the title – he was the new guy. But he does become a Musketeer by the end though.

Blast Off: The University of Toledo owes its nickname to a spur-of-the-moment decision that predates the space race. As the story goes, in 1923, Toledo student James Neal was working in the press box during a game at Carnegie Tech. Pittsburgh reporters demanded the school's nickname, which didn't exist. Tired of being browbeaten, Neal, who was watching his team get smacked 32–12, decided on the Skyrockets. Why? Because apparently losing by 20 still looks explosive if your opponent is good. The reporters trimmed it to **Rockets**, and somehow the name stuck, proving that nicknames age better than box scores.

Gold Mine: The Kent State football team did not score in its first three seasons (1920-22). In 1923, the team got a glow-up as the **Silver Foxes** – named after the president's nearby ranch – and finally scored in the first game. By 1926, a student naming contest gave rise to the **Golden Flashes**. A definition contest was not held, so people still aren't sure what the name means.

Learning to Fight: Central State University (Wilberforce) founding president, Dr. Charles H. Wesley, chose **Marauders** as the school's nickname and gold and maroon as the official colors in 1947. He envisioned the school as a haven for marauders or freedom fighters – using education to rescue and uplift their communities. Dr. Wesley explained that gold represented the wealth of knowledge. At the same time, maroon honored the Maroon settlements of freed people, like the one in Haiti, which defeated France and secured independence in 1802.

Letter Perfect: Oberlin College got its **Yeomen** nickname from football players in the early 1880s who earned a varsity letter "O." They were first called the Ye-O-Men, which eventually got smooshed into **Yeomen**. When women's athletics kicked off in 1973, they joined the pun parade as the **Yeowomen** because why let men have all the letter fun?

On the Dot: Script Ohio kicked off in 1936 when band director Eugene Weigel decided the Buckeye band's marching could use a little flair – like spelling and cursive writing. By 1937, sousaphone player Glen Johnson had turned it into a full-on spectacle: the band spells "Ohio" in script, a senior sousaphone struts up, high-fives the drum major, bows atop the "i," and claims the most famous tittle in the collegiate world. Even celebrities like Bob Hope and Jack Nicklaus have had their moment dotting the "i."

Spaced: The Capital University **Comets** (Columbus) went with some cosmic flair after being known as the **Crusaders** and the **Fighting Lutherans**.

Wise Choice: Kenyon College's (Gambier) nickname history has gone through plenty of changes. In 1880, the teams were called the **Mauve**, matching the school's original color. A shift to purple in the early 1930s brought about a new clever nickname: The **Purple**. Soon after, the school adopted the **Lords**, later the **Fighting Lords**, before switching to the **Pioneers** in 1940. Most recently, in 2022, Kenyon rebranded as the **Owls**, a nod to the Kokosing River that runs through campus. Its name translates roughly to "river of little owls."

Oklahoma

Cowboy Up: Oklahoma State's cowboy mascot, "Pistol Pete," is based on a Frank Eaton, a legendary U.S. marshal, author, and expert marksman. Eaton was given the nickname after winning a shooting contest at Fort Gibson.

In the early 1920s – when the school was known as the Oklahoma A&M **Aggies** – Eaton led Stillwater's Armistice Day Parade, and his distinct look caught the eye of some students. They asked if they could use him as a model for a new mascot. He agreed. And soon after, his likeness of a mustachioed cowboy ready to shoot was everywhere.

But Pistol Pete did not become the official mascot of the school until 1958 – a year after it became the Oklahoma State **Cowboys**. Pistol Pete is also the mascot for the University of Wyoming and New Mexico State because cowboys never retire.

Movin' On: The University of Science and Arts of Oklahoma (Chickasaw) is nicknamed the **Drovers** – the unsung heroes of the open range, whose job it was to drive cattle or sheep over long distances. These cowboys were part logistics managers and part sleep-deprived endurance athletes, often sporting cool hats.

On the Wagon: The University of Oklahoma (Norman) honors the 1889 Land Run by having the Sooner Schooner, a scaled-down Conestoga (covered wagon), pulled by white ponies named "Boomer" and "Sooner" who race across the field every time the football team scores. The Schooner was first introduced in 1964.

Over the Hill: Rogers State University (Claremore) and its predecessors have tried on numerous nicknames before settling on the **Hillcats** – a fictional cousin of the native bobcat, naturally chosen because the school is located on College Hill.

The institution's former identities include Oklahoma Military Academy **Cadets**, Claremore Junior College **Spartans**, and Rogers State College **Thunderbirds**. Apparently, consistency was never part of the curriculum.

Oregon

Early Bird: After the University of Oregon changed its nickname from **Webfoots** to **Ducks**. the school worked out a deal with Walt Disney to use Donald Duck's likeness as the mascot. Oregon calls it The Duck, but rivals insist the name is Puddles.

Time to Fly: The Columbia University **Cliffdwellers** are now known as the University of Portland **Pilots**.

Pennsylvania

Big Time: Keystone College (La Plume) is the **Giants** thanks to Hall of Fame pitcher Christy Mathewson. Before dominating professional baseball with the New York Giants, Mathewson pitched for Keystone Academy, the school's forerunner. When it came time for a nickname, the Giants connection was too good to pass up, even if they were borrowing from someone else's resume.

Crumbs of Tradition: University of Pennsylvania fans may be the only people on Earth who bring a loaf of bread to watch a football game. The ritual traces back to the school song *Drink a Highball* – accompanied initially by the school's unofficial cocktail called the Pennsylvanian. When Prohibition (and later, stadium rules) killed the booze, students got literal.

At the line "Here's a toast to dear old Penn," they started chucking actual toast onto the field. Some say the habit was reinforced in the 1970s by a *Rocky Horror* fan who thought, "Why not at football, too?" These days, the sidelines get carpeted in carbs – everything from bagels to baguettes.

Diplomatic Immunity: Franklin & Marshall College's (Lancaster) teams were once known by the clunky moniker **Nevoians**, which honored former school president John Williamson Nevin. By 1934, the student paper was tired of it and ran a contest looking for something better. Student Ira Honaman suggested "Diplomats," which the editors found so laughable that they published a satirical piece featuring players with briefcases and polite trash talk, before begging students to come up with literally anything else. The joke backfired. The administration loved it, and by the 1935 football season, Franklin & Marshall had officially become the **Diplomats**.

Flap Around: Saint Joseph's University (Philadelphia) doesn't just have a Hawk, it has the hardest-working mascot in college sports. Why? Because the student inside that feathery suit flaps nonstop. No breaks, no mercy, no "my arms are tired." At basketball games, that's over 3,500 flaps a night. And it's not just hoops – the Hawks' wings are flapping at fundraisers, press conferences, alumni mixers, and even weddings. Because who doesn't want to walk down the aisle with a sweaty college student in a bird costume flapping just a few feet away.

Going Dutch: The Lebanon Valley College **Flying Dutchmen** (Annvile) often leaves outsiders scratching their heads, imagining ghost ships when it's really a nod to Pennsylvania Dutch Country – Dutch being a bad translation of Deutsch (German).

The nickname traces back to 1932, when *Lebanon Daily News* columnist G.O. Gettum (yes, really) decided LVC needed to keep up with the Yales and Princetons of the world and put out a call for mascot suggestions.

The first idea? The Cedars, with a black cat mascot – an oddly prophetic choice, since a stray cat was literally found napping in Coach Hook Mylin's car the same week. Naturally, that was ignored. Instead, in a follow-up column, Gettum floated **Flying Dutchmen**, which Mylin loved – perhaps figuring it was safer to endorse the **Flying Dutchmen** than deal with actual Pennsylvania Dutchmen piling into his backseat.

Mixed-Up: The La Salle University **Explorers** (Philadelphia) is what happens when a couple of notable French guys get mixed up. The story goes that in 1931, while reporting on a football game, a local sportswriter jokingly referred to La Salle as the Explorers, thinking it had been named after the 17th-century French explorer who claimed the Mississippi River basin for France, René-Robert Cavelier, Sieur de La Salle.

Unfortunately for the reporter, the school was named after the French priest Jean Baptiste de La Salle. But it didn't matter to the students who voted for **Explorers** to be their nickname in 1932.

Old Money: Robert Morris University (Moon Township) is named the **Colonials** to honor its namesake, Founding Father Robert Morris, the man who was the financier of the American Revolution and signed every critical piece of parchment America had to offer – the Declaration of Independence, the Articles of Confederation, and the Constitution.

Straight Shooters: Gettysburg College athletes picked up the nickname **Bullets** in 1924 thanks to Paul Roy, a city editor with the *Gettysburg Times* and a flair for Civil War callbacks. After hearing football Coach Bill Wood speak at a dinner, Roy wrote an article about the school's connection to the Battle of Gettysburg, which occurred on the campus. He also compared players to ammunition, which hopefully reads better than it sounds.

Rhode Island

Bring to Bear: Brown University (Providence) wasn't thrilled with being called the **Hilltoppers** or the **Puritans**. In a moment of inspired desperation, a local real estate exec brought a burro all the way from Colorado Springs for a Harvard game – only to discover the donkey had zero interest in being there, tolerating rival fans, or becoming a mascot.

A few years later, Brown alum and future Rhode Island governor Theodore Francis Green mounted a bear head in the student union trophy room. Students decided that was way more intimidating than disgruntled burros or guys in funny hats, and **Bears** stuck.

Growing Admiration: There is no penis envy at the Rhode Island School of Design (Providence). It's all appreciation. The hockey team adopted the nickname **Nads** for the "Go **Nads**!" cheer. The basketball team is the **Balls**, and the fencing team is the **Pricks**. There are other teams as well, following the not-so-subtle theme.

South Carolina

Cock of the Walk: The South Carolina **Gamecocks** strut their stuff with Sir Big Spur VII, a live Old English Black Breasted Red Fighting Gamecock, alongside the costumed mascot Cocky. At one point, administrators tried to retire the Sir Big Spur name in favor of The General, honoring Revolutionary War hero Thomas Sumter. A newspaper poll begged to differ, favoring Cock Commander, but in the end, tradition (and maybe some stubbornness) won out.

Knight Moves: In 1961, Furman decided that Purple Hurricanes (football), **Harriers** (track), and **Hornets** (baseball) didn't make sense to have at the same time.

Thanks to a student vote, all Furman sports teams were unified under the banner of the **Paladins** or **Purple Paladins**, a nod to the legendary knights of Charlemagne's court – because nothing says college athletics like medieval chivalry.

Namely: Today, North Greenville (Tigerville) is the **Trailblazers**. Previously, the school was known as the **Moonshiners**, **Black Widow Spiders**, **Mountaineers**, and **Crusaders**, illustrating that choosing a collegiate nickname can be a wild ride.

Up in the Air: Erskine College (Due West) started as the **Seceders** before changing to the **Flying Fleet** in 1929. The convoy nickname came from Greenville News sportswriter Carter "Scoop" Latimer, who described the team's passing attack against Furman as such in a game story. Students voted **Flying Fleet** in as the new nickname months later.

Rock Solid: Clemson's run down The Hill – the so-called "most exciting 25 seconds in college football" – began in 1942, when the Tigers' locker room sat atop The Hill and players jogged down to the field. In 1966, a booster mounted a rock from California's Death Valley that longtime Coach Frank Howard had received years earlier at the top. The coach had previously used it as a doorstop, but once players started rubbing "Howard's Rock" for good luck in 1967, a ritual that began before a 23–6 win over Wake Forest was born. More than 440 sprints later, the ritual proves that one man's doorstop can become a college's sacred tradition.

South Dakota

Bunny Hop: South Dakota State's **Jackrabbits** (Brookings) nickname has two origin stories. The most common says it started after a 1905 football game against Minnesota, when a Minneapolis reporter described the players as "quick as jackrabbits." The name stuck, and many believe it became the school's identity from that point forward.

The second theory originates from the 1907 yearbook, *The Jackrabbit*, when a group of juniors renamed the annual to immortalize themselves, and the athletic teams simply followed their lead.

Heavy Metal: The South Dakota School of Mines and Technology **Hardrockers** (Rapid City) rock a nickname that pays homage to the university, which was initially founded in 1885 as a mining school. Bang your head!

Tennessee

Full Steam Ahead: The Vanderbilt University **Commodores** (Nashville) takes its nickname from its founder, Cornelius Vanderbilt, who got the nickname "Commodore" as a tough, ambitious steamboat operator running ferries between Manhattan and Staten Island.

From the Ashes: Cumberland University (Lebanon) spent years letting its teams bark as the **Bulldogs** while its stained-glass windows, logos, and school lore screamed phoenix. The bird came from the Civil War, after the campus burned to the ground in 1863, and only two Corinthian columns survived. The school was rebuilt, but it took until 2016 for it to finally notice the obvious.

After a lot of time awkwardly explaining why their **Bulldogs** wore bird insignias, Cumberland made it official: The **Phoenix** was free to soar officially.

On the Fence: Like the name of the school, the **Railsplitters** of Lincoln Memorial University (Harrogate) also honor former U.S. President Abraham Lincoln. A railsplitter is a person who splits logs into rails, usually for building fences, which Lincoln had done in his youth. Lincoln was called "The Railsplitter" in May 1860 by Illinois Republicans who thought "Honest Abe" needed a better nickname to get elected.

Strength in Numbers: The University of Tennessee (Knoxville) may have the record for the most official mascots. A student dresses as folk hero Davy Crockett, with a rifle and coonskin cap, to represent the volunteer spirit of the state.

There's also Smokey – a real dog. In 1953, the school marched out 10 canines at halftime of a football game and had fans clap for their favorite. A bluetick coonhound howled for acceptance and won the crowd over.

Since then, 11 Smokeys have represented the school. There is also a costumed Smokey, who first made an appearance in 1973. Faux Smokey has been joined by his younger brother, parents, and grandparents for special occasions, which can make for a very crowded sideline.

We're Number One: Austin Peay State University (Clarksville) named its teams the **Governors** after Tennessee Governor Austin Peay (pronounced like black-eyed pea), who also lent his name to the school. The result? One of college sports' greatest chants: "Let's Go Peay!" – a rallying cry that never stops sounding like bathroom humor disguised as school spirit.

Texas

Almost Ferrets: Baylor University (Waco) didn't have an official mascot until 1914, when the school president decided it was time for an identity. Students voted, and despite stiff competition from over two dozen contenders – including Buffaloes, Antelopes, Frogs, and Ferrets – the students chose the **Bears**.

Bugle Call: In January 1931, a group of Texas A&M (College Station) cadets hit a stray dog with their vehicle on the way back to campus. They scooped her up and hid her in their dorm – pets were not allowed – to nurse her back to health. Their secret was found out when a bugler played Reveille early the next morning, and the dog started barking up a storm. Her name was an obvious choice. Reveille became so popular with the students that she was named the school's official mascot at the beginning of the 1931 football season. Since Reveille III took over in 1966, all the mascots have been purebred Rough Collies.

Carb Bombs: In the early 1990s, Texas Tech fans decided the best way to show school spirit was to turn their stadium into the world's weirdest Tex-Mex restaurant. The most popular theory as to why they started to fling tortillas is when an ESPN announcer mocked Lubbock as having "nothing but Texas Tech football and a tortilla factory" in 1992. Instead of being insulted, fans showed up at the next game with bags of tortillas and launched them at kickoff. Three decades later, it's still raining carbs because you can't have football in West Texas without airborne flatbread.

Creature Komforts: Sam Houston State University (Huntsville) ditched the **Normals** in 1923 for something lifted from a local saying – "tough as a Bearcat!" Because it was more of a mythical beast than a real creature, the school settled on a quirky spelling – **Bearkats**. In the late 1940s, the school president tried to rebrand to the Ravens, a nod to Sam Houston's Cherokee nickname, probably because he was tired of telling people, "k instead of a c." The **Bearkats** held on – proving once again, a good legend doesn't care about spelling.

Digging In: When the State School of Mines and Metallurgy opened in 1914, the football team was called the **Miners** – because, well, subtlety wasn't really the priority. The name stuck even as the school's identity went through a full-on rebrand marathon: College of Mines and Metallurgy, El Paso in 1919, Texas Western College in 1949, and finally the University of Texas at El Paso in 1967. Through all the name changes, at least the **Miners** didn't have to keep buying new jerseys.

Hold Your Horses: Texas Tech's (Lubbock) live mascot began as a 1936 dare: a ghost rider – cloaked in a mask and a cape galloped around the field and then vanished like a supernatural cowboy. By 1954, the Masked Rider became official, and ever since, this mysterious equestrian has proudly led the football team onto the field, proving that some heroes don't need a cape – just a darn good horse.

Hop to It: Austin College (Sherman) wound up with the **Kangaroos** as its mascot, though no one can quite agree on why. One tale claims Rice University's coach in 1912 said the team was "as fast as kangaroos" after getting obliterated 81–0.

The more likely origin? Back when Austin College was an all-male military school, it had a freshman hazing tradition known as the "Kangaroo Court." By 1913, the military drills were gone, but the kangaroo stuck around – because who doesn't like to incorporate school spirit with freshman hazing.

Pony Up: In 1917, Southern Methodist University (Dallas) held a campus vote to pick a mascot, with **Mustangs** galloping past Bison, Greyhounds, and Pioneers. Their live mascot arrived in 1932 – a black Shetland pony named Peruna, named after a Prohibition-era "medicinal tonic" that was 18 percent alcohol and marketed as "full of kick."

As for the legend that the Mustang car got its name because Ford's Lee Iacocca watched SMU lose to Michigan in 1963 and then strolled into the locker room to announce it? Great story. But devotees are probably backing the wrong horse.

Needs A Lot: In 1946, the University of Houston's Alpha Phi Omega fraternity raised funds to bring a live cougar to campus – and naturally held a naming contest. The winning entry? Shasta, with the explanation: "Shasta (she has to). Shasta have a cage,

Shasta have a keeper, Shasta have a winning ball club, Shasta have the best." Clearly, Shasta was expected to multitask.

Quack Attack: The College of the Mainland (Texas City) experienced an identity crisis regarding its nicknames. In 1968, they were the **Comets**; then, in 1973, they became the **Fighting Comets**. In 1976, they were known as the **Mainland Comets**, and by 1977, they had no nickname at all. Fast forward to 2006, students voted, and the winner was the **Fighting Ducks** – because apparently, hostile birds were a perfect fit.

Rebranding: The University of Texas (Austin) has had a live longhorn mascot since the mid-1910s. Texas A&M students say the steer got its name after some **Aggie** pranksters branded it 13-0, the score of the 1915 game. Then Texas students altered the brand by making the "13" into a "B", the "-" into an "E", inserting a "V" before the "0," creating the name Bevo.

The **Longhorn** faithful disagree. They say a writer created the name to mark Texas' 21-7 win over A&M in 1916, which featured a longhorn being led onto the field at halftime. The next issue of *Texas Exes Alcalde* magazine included a summary of the contest, where editor Ben Dyer said, "His name is Bevo. Long may he reign." There are some theories as to where Dyer got the name, including that "beeve" is the plural of "beef," and how people in those days liked to add an "o" to the end of names. Add an "o" to your spouse's name and see if it improves the relationship.

Standing Room Only: In 1922, Texas A&M (College Station) players were getting pummeled, bruised, and bloodied by the highly ranked Centre College **Praying Colonels** in the Dixie Classic. Coach Dana X. Bible looked at his sideline and realized he was about to be short on players. Enter E. King Gill, a former member of the football team and current **Aggie** basketball player, who was up in the press box helping to identify players for reporters. Bible got Gill down to the sideline, so he, too, could be hurt if needed. Gill suited up in the uniform of injured running back Heine Weir and stood ready to go in just in case more players limped off the field.

A&M pulled off the monumental upset 22–14. Gill never got into the game, but his readiness to play turned into the **Aggie** tradition known as the 12th Man. And now every **Aggie** student stands for the whole contest just in case they are needed (about 38,000 at home games) – because of the actions of the most celebrated human insurance policy in Texas A&M history.

Tusky Business: Texas A&M–Kingsville is the only U.S. university to boast the **Javelinas** as a mascot – not a pig, not a feral hog, but a collared peccary, a distant cousin of the hippo with a serious attitude problem when cornered. The school's first students picked the javelina for its fierce reputation, and sure, those two-inch canine teeth can do real damage, but in reality, it would much rather run than rumble.

Rivalries
Games & Trophies

- **100 Miles of Hate** - Middle Tennessee vs. W. Kentucky
- **Apple Cup** - Washington vs Washington State
- **Backyard Brawl** - Pittsburgh vs. West Virginia
- **Battle for the Bones** - Memphis vs. UAB
- **Battle for the Iron Skillet** - SMU vs. TCU
- **Battle of I-10** - New Mexico State vs. UTEP
- **Battle of the Brazos** - Baylor vs. Texas A&M
- **Battle of the Brothers** - Utah vs. Utah State
- **Bayou Bucket** - Houston vs. Rice
- **Bayou Classic** - Grambling State vs. Southern
- **Bedlam** - Oklahoma vs. Oklahoma State
- **Big Game** - California vs. Stanford
- **Black Hills Brawl** - Black Hills State vs. SD Mines
- **Bluebonnet Battle** - Baylor vs. TCU
- **Border War** - Colorado State vs. Wyoming
- **Border War** - Kansas vs. Missouri
- **Brawl of the Wild** - Montana vs. Montana State
- **Bronze Stalk** - Ball State vs. Northern Illinois
- **Cereal Bowl** - Carleton vs. St. Olaf
- **Dog Fight** - Minnesota-Duluth vs. St. Cloud State
- **Duel in the Desert** - Arizona vs. Arizona State
- **Egg Bowl** - Mississippi State vs. Mississippi

- **Farmageddon** - Iowa State vs. Kansas State
- **Floyd of Rosedale** - Iowa vs. Minnesota
- **Holy War** - BYU vs. Utah
- **Iron Bowl** - Alabama vs Auburn
- **Keg of Nails** - Cincinnati vs. Louisville
- **Land of Lincoln** - Illinois vs. Northwestern
- **Little Brown Jug** - Michigan vs. Minnesota
- **Lone Star Showdown** - Texas vs. Texas A&M
- **Magnolia Bowl** - LSU vs. Mississippi
- **Modern Day Hate** - Ga. Southern vs. Ga. State
- **Oil Can** - Fresno State vs. San Diego State
- **Old Brass Spittoon** - Indiana vs. Michigan State
- **Old Oaken Bucket** - Indiana vs. Purdue
- **Paint Bucket Bowl** - Arkansas State vs. Memphis
- **Paul Bunyan Trophy** - Michigan vs. Michigan State
- **Paul Bunyan's Axe** - Minnesota vs. Wisconsin
- **Platypus Trophy** - Oregon vs. Oregon State
- **Purdue Cannon** - Purdue vs. Illinois
- **Red River Rivalry** - Oklahoma vs. Texas
- **Rumble in the Rockies** - Colorado vs. Utah
- **Secretary's Trophy** - Army vs. Navy
- **Soul Bowl** - Alcorn State vs. Jackson State
- **Sunflower Showdown** - Kansas vs. Kansas State
- **The Game** - Harvard vs. Yale
- **The Game** - Michigan vs. Ohio State
- **The Rivalry** - Lafayette vs. Lehigh

Utah

Changing Pace: The Westminster College **Purps** (Salt Lake City) are now known as the Westminster College **Griffins**.

Clawed Into Existence: Weber State (Ogden) didn't pick **Wildcats** with a student vote – it came from a locker room trash talk in the 1920s. When a teammate mocked another for playing like a "pussycat" at practice, captain Monk Holliday shot back, "He's no pussycat, he's a Wildcat!"

Wally Morris was now known as Wildcat Morris, and soon after, a local sportswriter spread the name to the whole team, and the nickname **Weberites** was history.

For a while, the school even paraded a live wildcat at games – until one took its version of trash talk too far and bit a cheerleader on the nose.

Fountain of Ute: The University of Utah's (Salt Lake City) athletic teams take their name from the Ute tribe, the Indigenous people for whom the state itself is named.

The Utes, or *Nuche* (The People), have lived in the region for more than a thousand years and were among the first Native nations to adopt the horse. The school works in partnership with the Ute Tribal Business Committee to carry the **Utes** as a nickname.

Vermont

Claws of Democracy: In 1926, University of Vermont (Burlington) students held a vote to pick a nickname, and **Catamounts** narrowly clawed past the Lynx. Other options? Cows, Camels, Tom-Cats, or just giving up and having no mascot at all. The **Catamounts** were a solid choice, but the Fighting Cows would have turned some heads.

Name Calling: The Saint Michael's College **Purple Knights** (Colchester) were formerly known as the **Michaelmen**.

Virginia

Exit Light: When Virginia Tech got its first video board in 2000, they needed a killer entrance soundtrack for the **Hokies** football team. The finalists? *Enter Sandman (*Metallica*), Welcome to the Jungle,*(Guns N' Roses), and *Sirius* (Alan Parsons Project).

Metallica won, and heavy metal soon became a staple of college football. The first time the song was supposed to rock Lane Stadium, the heavens apparently weren't ready. Thunderstorms rolled in, the game was canceled, and ESPN's Lee Corso even had his rental car struck by lightning. Since then, the Hokies have been sleeping with one eye open.

For a Song: The University of Virginia (Charlottesville) has a history of nicknames for its athletic teams, including **Cavaliers**, **Wahoos**, **Hoos**, and a few others. Legend says Washington & Lee baseball fans first called Virginia players **Wahoos** in the 1890s, and by 1940, it was in general circulation around campus. Meanwhile, *The Cavalier Song* flopped soon after winning the 1923 contest for the school fight song – but somehow gave rise to the **Cavaliers** nickname.

Keyed Up: The Virginia Military Institute (Lexington) somehow ended up with the nickname **Keydets** – a moniker whose origin is lost to history. Some say it nods to the gray cadet uniforms; others claim Southern accents turned "cadet" into "Keydet." Whatever the truth, it replaced the **Flying Squadron** in the early 1930s, and today a kangaroo mascot named TD Bound represents all that disciplined confusion.

Tight Ship: The Apprentice School **Builders** (Newport News) constructs ships. Founded in 1919, the vocational school is operated by the Newport News Shipbuilding & Dry Dock Company and trains students for careers in shipbuilding and other skilled trades. It fields seven athletic teams.

Towel Off: In 1947, James Madison University's (Harrisonburg) first men's basketball team promised they would name themselves the **Dukes** after school President Samuel P. Duke – if he supplied towels and equipment. Because when you're building a legacy, don't forget the laundry service.

Web Surfing: The University of Richmond ditched the **Colts** nickname in 1894 with a bit of help in realizing that adorable horses didn't capture the baseball team's vibe.

Puss Ellyson, a lanky pitcher whose freakishly long arms and legs made batters look like they were swatting at invisible bugs, was dominating the competition. So a local sportswriter dubbed the team the **Spiders**, and just like that, Richmond was known as eight-legged terrors – because why be cute when you can be terrifyingly awkward?

Washington

Change Up: Washington State (Pullman) tried on a whole closet full of nicknames in the early years - **Farmers**, **Aggies**, **Hayseeds**, and **Potato Diggers** (All for root vegetables, stand up and holler!).

By 1912, with three consecutive football coaches arriving from the Carlisle Indian School, the teams cycled through **Indians**, **Chiefs**, and **Braves**. Then, on October 25, 1919, when WSU played the University of California, Berkley, a cartoonist doodled them as **Cougars**, or a columnist said they fought like **Cougars**. The students shrugged and said, "Yeah, that works." By October 28, it was a done deal. By November 1, the school had already paraded out two stuffed **Cougars** at a football game against Idaho – because nothing says it's official like taxidermy official.

Ray of Light: The University of Washington (Seattle) was the **Sundodgers** for two years before becoming the **Huskies** in 1922. Local businesses and newspapers demanded the change, feeling the nickname was an unfair representation of the city's weather.

Tree Huggers: The Gray Harbor College **Chokers** (Aberdeen) nickname is not a commentary on their performance under pressure, but instead a call out to the area's logging industry. A choker (a cable or chain) is wrapped around logs so they can be hauled out of the forest. The person who performs this dangerous job is a choke setter, which is where the nickname originates. NFL Hall of Famer John Madden played for the **Chokers** in 1956.

Washington, D.C.

Strong Language: When Georgetown University was known as the **Stonewalls**, the students created a cheer using Greek and Latin. Translated, "Hoya Saxa!" means "What rocks!" and became so popular across campus that **Hoyas** became the nickname in 1926.

West Virginia

For the Birds: The West Virginia Northern Community College **Thundering Chickens** (Wheeling) is a nickname without a reason. Did it rain chickens? Were there large chickens? Were there noisy chickens? No one is saying, leaving us thunderstruck.

Rugged: The West Virginia University **Mountaineers** nickname is derived from West Virginia being the Mountain State. Since 1934, a buckskin-clad mascot – today a **Mountaineer** with a musket and a coonskin cap – has represented the school at major events.

Sing It: West Virginia University (Morgantown) fans have been belting out *Take Me Home, Country Roads* at every home pregame and after every win since 1972. John Denver's 1971 hit, which climbed all the way to No. 2 on the Billboard charts, quickly became the school's unofficial anthem as well as the go-to sing-along at stadiums across the world. Because, as the **Mountaineers** already know, it's fun to sing about West Virginia.

Stampede of Confusion: Marshall University's (Huntington) nickname saga is a long and winding one. The school started as the **Indians** before 1900, shifted to **Big Green** around 1910, and then, in the late 1920s, a sportswriter likened the football team to a **Thundering Herd** (because he liked the movie based on a Zane Grey book with that name). And the moniker sort of stuck.

But some folks balked: "Do you know where we are? What's thundering exactly?" Others pitched Boogercats, inspired by Scotland's fleet and courageous Bogie Cats, though it predominantly just conjured up nightmares. Even turkeys – promoted as the Green Gobblers – got some momentum. By the 1960s, the student body decided enough was enough: **Thundering Herd** it is, complete with a buffalo mascot, while Big Green became the athletic fundraising group's moniker. All the others were sent to the dustbin of history – until next time.

Wisconsin

Catch of the Day: Lakeland College (Sheboygan) owes its nickname to athletic director Elmer Ott, who in the 1930s had to think of a nickname for the school's teams. Instead of looking to history, mythology, or school spirit, he went straight to his tackle box. He thought about the fish that gave him the most trouble – the mighty muskellunge. So, the school became the **Muskies**.

Sleeping Arrangements: The University of Wisconsin **Badgers** (Madison) nickname is derived from Wisconsin being known as the Badger State. That nickname refers to the lead miners who worked in Wisconsin and had to stay in their tunnels during the winter months for shelter – living like badgers.

Four schools outside of Wisconsin have the Badgers nickname. None of them gets their name from mining or living like badgers.

Up and Down: In 1998, Wisconsin football needed a boost, so an injured tight end and his buddies handed the marketing team a hype-song playlist. On it? House of Pain's 1992 banger *Jump Around*. The next game, it was blasted on the stadium speakers between the third and fourth quarters against Purdue, and even though Wisconsin was losing, the students started bouncing like pogo sticks on espresso. Ever since, 80,000 fans at Camp Randall have been shaking the stadium's foundation at every game.

Wyoming

Cowboy Up: The University of Wyoming got its **Cowboys** nickname in 1891 before the school had even played an official football game. The story goes that a club squad at the school, short on muscle, recruited a 220-pound cowpuncher named Fred Bush to face off against the Cheyenne Soldiers. Bush signed up for a couple of classes (you know, for eligibility's sake), then strutted onto the field in a checkered shirt and cowboy hat. Someone in the crowd shouted, "Hey, look at the Cowboy!" and just like that, Wyoming had a nickname.

Quick Study: The Gillette College **Pronghorns** are the only school to honor the fastest land animal in North America.

Conclusion

You've made your way from **Aardvarks** to **Zippers**, travelled across the country, and read about some trends and traditions along the way.

So whether you represent the Brazosport College **Gators** (Lake Jackson, TX), cheer for the Alverno **Inferno** (Milwaukee, WI), or have questions about the Webster University **Gorloks** (St. Louis, MO), you hopefully know more today about collegiate nicknames than when you started.

The quest to find the Fighting Giraffes continues ...

Notes

Akron Zips
- *What is a Zip, and why is Akron's mascot a kangaroo?* beaconjournal.com (April 25, 2025)

Alabama Crimson Tide
- Chris Mahr. *The story behind Alabama's elephant mascot.* sports.yahoo.com/blogs/ (Oct. 23, 2012)
- *How the Crimson Tide Got its Name.* rolltide.com
- Andy Wittry. *How Alabama got the nickname 'Crimson Tide'.* ncaa.com (Sept. 13, 2022)
- John Duffley. *Why 'Dixieland Delight' Is a Timeless yet Controversial Alabama Football Tradition.* fanbuzz.com (Nov. 2, 2023)
- *The Elephant Story.* rolltide.com

Alaska-Anchorage Sourdoughs
- Bailey Berg. *Why Longtime Alaska Residents Are Called 'Sourdoughs'.* atlasobscura.com (Jan. 15, 2021)
- *What is a Seawolf.* uaa.alaska.edu (April 23, 2013)

Albion College Britons
- Andrew Wittland. *Why the Briton?* albionpleiad.com (Oct. 16, 2015)

Alma College Scots
- *Our Story.* alma.edu

Amherst College Mammoths
- *Amherst College replaces Lord Jeff mascot with Mammoths.* Associated Press. (April 4, 2017)
- *Amherst College Story.* pentagram.com

Arizona State Sun Devils
- Brad Hall. *How Arizona State University Became the Sun Devils.* dieharddevil.com (April 26, 2015)

Arizona Wildcats
- *Mascot History.* arizonawildcats.com. (March 31, 2009)

Arkansas Monticello Boll Weevils
- Julie Kohl. *The History of Arkansas Mascots.* onlyinark.com (Oct. 31, 2016)

Arkansas Razorbacks
- Reagan Netherland. *Hog History: How the Razorback became the University of Arkansas' mascot.* uatrav.com (Aug. 28, 2024)

Arkansas Tech Wonder Boys
- *98 Years of Wonder Boys: Origin Story.* arkansastechnews.com (Nov. 16, 2018)

Army Black Knights
- *Army Mules.* goarmysports.com (Aug. 25, 2011)

Auburn Tigers
- *Auburn Traditions.* auburn.edu
- *Rolling Toomer's Corner.* auburntigers.com

Austin College Kangaroos
- Marc Parrish. *Origin Story: The History of the Kangaroo Mascot.* roonation.org (Nov. 29, 2016)

Austin Peay Governors
- *About Austin Peay.* letsgopeay.com

Ave Maria Gyrenes
- *What is a Gyrene?* avemariagyrenes.com

Ball State Cardinals
- *History of the Ball State Cardinals Mascot.* collegefooootballnetwork.com. (March 20, 2023)

Baylor Bears
- *The Bear Nickname and Mascot.* baylorbears.com

Bemidji State University Beavers
- *It's International Beaver Day! Do you know the history of Bemidji State's favorite mascot* bsualumni.org. (April 7, 2025)

Bethany College Swedes
- *Heritage & Traditions.* bethanylb.edu

Bethel Threshers
- *What is a Thresher?* bethelks.edu

Bethune-Cookman Wildcats
- *#MaryMemories: Dr. Bethune and the Wildcats Mascot.* bcuathletics.com (July 8, 2013)

Boston University Terriers
- *Rhett the Terrier, through the Years.* bu.edu. (March 19, 2018)

Bowdoin College Polar Bears
- *The Bowdoin Polar Bear.* athletics.dowdoin.edu

Brewton-Parker Christian Barons
- *What is a Baron?* bpcuathletics.com

Brooklyn College Bridges
- Shea Stevenson. *Opinion: Bring Back The Brooklyn Bridges*. vanguard.blog.brooklyn.edu. (Feb. 15, 2023)

Brown University Bears
- Peter Mackie. *And the Bear Growls*. 250.brown.edu

Butler Bulldogs
- *Butler Blue: Official Butler University Mascots*. blogs.butler.edu

BYU-Idaho Mighty Oaks
- Justin Hodges. *Becoming Mighty Oaks*. byui.edu. (Nov. 20, 2018)

Cal Poly Maritime Keelhaulers
- *Definition of a Keelhauler*. gokeelhaulers.com

Campbell University Fighting Camels
- Billy Liggett. *Why the Camels?* magazine.campbell.edu. (June 4, 2019)

Catawba College Catawba Indians
- *Catawba College Sideline Mascot*. catawba.edu

Central Arkansas Sugar Bears
- *UCA Mascots*. ucasports.com

Central State Marauders
- *History of Logo & Colors*. maraudersports.com

Centre College Praying Colonels
- *Chapter 2*. centrewonderteam.com
- *Hall of Fame*. centrecolonels.com

Chaminade University Silverswords
- *What is a Silversword?* goswords.com

Chesapeake College Skipjacks
- *Skipjacks*. mdsg.umd.edu

Chico State Wildcats
- *The Wildcat*. csuchico.edu

Cincinnati Bearcats
- Cedric Ricks. *A century-old love affair with the Bearcat*. uc.edu. (May 31, 2024)

Clemson Tigers
- Darrian Carter. *Why does Clemson football run down the hill? Explaining history of Tigers' tradition*. Greenville News. (Aug. 20, 2025)

- Jay Coulter. *History Surrounds Auburn-Clemson Series*. collegeandmagnolia.com. (Sept. 13, 2010)

Coastal Carolina Chanticleers
- Jack McKessy. *What is a Chanticleer? Coastal Carolina's mascot explained*. USA Today. (May 31, 2025)

Colby College Mules
- *Making of the Mule: How Colby's Mascot Came to Life*. colbyathletics.com. (March 26, 2021)

College of the Mainland Fighting Ducks
- *COM History*. libguides.com.edu/COMHistory

College of the Redwoods
- Dylan McNeill. *CR to go by 'Redwoods' after deliberating mascot change*. Times Standard. (June 26, 2025)

Colorado Buffaloes
- *Ralphie History*. cubuffs.com

Colorado School of Mines Orediggers
- *Blaster the Burro*. minesathletics.com

Colorado State Rams
- *Colorado State Rams' Mascot History*. collegefootballnetwork.com. (Aug. 17, 2024)

Columbia Lions
- *Columbia Athletics Tradition*. gocolumbialions.com

Community Colleges of Spokane Sasquatches
- Tim Binnall. *College Makes Odd Cryptid Mascot Swap*. (Jan. 23, 2025)

Concordia College Cobbers
- *Tradition of "Cobber"*. gocobbers.com

Connecticut College Camels
- Sarah Haughey. *What's With The Camel? The Real Story Behind The Conn Mascot*. thecollegevoice.org (Oct. 3, 2009)

Cornell Big Red
- *Cornell Traditions*. cornellbigred.com

Cumberland Phoenix
- Mike Organ. *Bulldogs out, Phoenix in as Cumberland sports nickname*. The Tennessean. (Jan. 4, 2016)
- *The Legacy of the Phoenix*. thinningcrowd.com.

Dartmouth Big Green
- *Keggy*. sites.dartmouth.edu

Dayton Flyers
- Eli Powell. *The Dayton Flyers*. thelowmajor.substack.com (Jan. 10, 2023)

Delaware Blue Hens
- Andrea Boyle Tippett. *Why Blue Hens?* udel.edu. (March 11, 2022)

Delta State University Fighting Okra
- Wayne Cavadi. *Just what is a Fighting Okra?* ncaa.com (May 30, 2017)

Dickinson State Blue Hawks
- *History of DSU*. dickinsonstate.edu

Duke Blue Devils
- *The Duke Blue Devil*. goduke.com

Emory & Henry Wasps
- *Why are Emory & Henry teams called the Wasps?* gowasps.com

Enterprise State Boll Weevils
- Lorraine Boissoneault. *Why an Alabama Town Has a Monument Honoring the Most Destructive Pest in American History*. smithsonianmag.com (May 31, 2017)

Erskine Flying Fleet
- *What are the Flying Fleet?* erskinesports.com

Evansville Purple Aces
- *Purple Aces & Ace Purple*. gopurpleaces.com

Evergreen State Geoducks
- *Our Mascot*. evergreen.edu

Fairfield Stags
- *Fairfield Stags*. logos-world.net/fairfield-stags-logo. (June 27, 2025)

Felician University Golden Falcons
- *Radio Felician Goes One on One with Bob Symons*. felician.edu

Five Towns College Sound
- *Fast Facts*. ftc.edu

Florida A&M Rattlers
- John Marsh. *Rattler mascot's origins unknown*. thefamuanonline.com (Oct. 5, 2025)

Florida Gators
- *The Birth of a Nickname*. floridagators.com

Florida State Seminoles
- Kani Schram. *Unconquered: The history of Osceola and Renegade*. fsunews.com (Jan. 2, 2025)
- *The Sod Cemetery*. seminoles.com
- *The Unconquered People*. seminoles.com

Franklin & Marshall Diplomats
- Jill Colford Schoeniger. *Why the Diplomats?* godiplomats.com

Furman Paladins
- *Furman Paladin*. libguides.furman.edu.

Gaston College Rhinos
- Bill Poteat. *Rhinos taking charge at Gaston College*. gastongazette.com (Aug. 20, 2021)

Georgetown Hoyas
- *What is a Hoya?* guhoyas.com

Georgia Bulldogs
- *Georgia Bulldogs Traditions*. georgiadogs.com.
- *Uga - The Georgia Mascot*. georgiadogs.com

Georgia Tech Yellow Jackets
- *Buzz*. traditions.gatech.edu
- *The Ramblin' Wreck*. traditions.gatech.edu

Gettysburg College Bullets
- *History & Traditions*. gettysburgsports.com

Gogebic Community College Samsons
- *Sam the Samson*. gogebic.edu

Goldey-Beacom College Lightning
- *History*. gbc.edu

Grays Harbor Chokers
- *Mascot Charlie Choker*. ghc.edu

Great Falls College River Otters
- Colter Anstaett. *Great Falls College-MSU now has a mascot*. krtv.com. (Feb. 7, 2023)

Gulf Coast State College Commodores
- *History of Gulf Coast State College*. gulfcoast.edu

Hameline University Pipers
- Cassie Willaert. *Hamline Piper M.I.A*. hamlineoracle.com (Nov. 13, 2018)

Harding Bisons
- *We are the Bisons*. hardingsports.com

Hawai'i-Hilo Vulcans
- Trixie Croad. *Editorial: What is a Vulcan?* hilo.hawaii.edu

Hawaii Rainbow Warriors
- *UH Traditions.* hawaiiathletics.com

Heidelberg University Student Princes
- *The Student Prince.* bergathletics.com

Henderson State Reddies
- *What is a Reddie?* hsusports.com

Hillsdale College Chargers
- Shane Armstrong. *Hillsdale did not always charge on.* hillsdalecollegian.com (Oct. 10, 2013)

Houston Cougars
- Alveena Rehlman. *Shasta: The History of The Cougar Mascot.* cooglife.com. (May 6, 2024)

Huntington University Foresters
- *Meet Norm the Forester.* huathletics.com

Idaho State Bengals
- *Traditions.* isubengals.com

Idaho Vandals
- *The Story of Joe Vandal.* govandals.com

Illinois Fighting Illini
- Sam Jarden. *What is an Illini? Explaining the origin of Illinois' nickname, mascot history.* sportingnews.com (March 16, 2023)

Illinois State Salukis
- *What's a Saluki?* siusalukis.com

Indiana Hoosiers
- Dan Treacy. *What is a Hoosier? Explaining the origin of Indiana's nickname, mascot history.* sportingnews.com (March 17, 2023)

Indiana University Southeast Grenadiers
- *History and Traditions.* southeast.iu.edu

Iowa Hawkeyes
- *Hawkeye Traditions.* oniowa.uiowa.edu

Iowa State Cyclones
- Matthew Voelker. *Why is Iowa State Called the Cyclones?* clutchbuzz.bet. (Dec. 30, 2022)

Iowa Western Reivers
- *What is a Reiver?* iwcc.edu

Ithaca Bombers
- *Why are Ithaca College athletic teams called the Bombers?* libanswers.ithaca.edu

Jacksonville State Gamecocks
- *Why We Are the Gamecocks.* jaxstatesports.com

James Madison Dukes
- *Dukes Nickname and the Duke Dog.* jmu.edu

John Brown University Golden Eagles
- Jeff Eisenberg. *The World-Famous Toilet Paper Game.* jbuathletics.com (Nov. 2, 2011)

Kansas Jayhawks
- Joe Kozlowski. *What is a Jayhawk, and what does it have to do with the University of Kansas?* sportscasting.com

Kent State Golden Flashes
- Jan Senn. *Forerunners of Flash.* kent.edu

Kentucky Wildcats
- *UK Traditions.* ukalumni.net

Kenyon College Owls
- *Kenyon College changes nickname to Owls.* mountvernonnews.com (June 13, 2022)

Keystone College Giants
- Tom Haley. *A little school with big baseball history.* rutlandherald.com (April 17, 2025)

Knox College Prairie Fire
- *History of a nickname and a nickname change.* qconline.com (Nov. 29, 2005)

La Salle Explorers
- Richard Smith. *Tom Gola Arena – La Salle Explorers.* stadiumjourney.com. (May 8, 2022)

Lakeland College Muskies
- Karla Ceja. *The Story Behind Our Muskie's Fighting Spirit.* lakelandmirror.com. (March 8, 2022)

Lebanon Valley College Flying Dutchman
- Harry Speece. *The Flying Dutchmen.* godutchmen.com

Lincoln Memorial University Railsplitters
- *What is a Railsplitter?* lmurailsplitters.com

Long Beach State Dirtbags
- Jeff Blank. *What Does A Baseball Dirtbag Mean?* sportslawblogger.com (May 8, 2024)

Louisiana-Lafayette Ragin' Cajuns
- *What is the Name?* ragincajuns.com

Louisiana Tech Lady Techsters
- Jim Rapier. *Sonja Hogg built the Louisiana Tech women's basketball program into a powerhouse.* New Orleans Times-Picayune. (June 24, 2009)

Loyola of Chicago Ramblers
- *Traditions: Why Ramblers?* loyolaramblers.com

LSU Tigers
- *Facts about Mike.* www.lsu.edu
- *LSU's Live Tiger Mascot: Mike VII.* lsusports.net

LSU-Alexandria Generals
- *Tank's Traditions.* lsua.edu

Maine Black Bears
- *How UMaine's mascot went from a bear to a moose and back to a bear.* dailymainer.com (Dec. 13, 2022)

Manhattan College Jaspers
- *What is a Jasper?* gojaspers.com

Manhattanville University Valiants
- *What is a Valiant?* govaliants.com

Marshall Thundering Herd
- *Why The Thundering Herd?* herdzone.com

Mary Baldwin Fighting Squirrels
- *The Fighting Squirrels.* marybaldwinathletics.com

Massachusetts Minutemen
- *Traditions: Why the Minutemen?* umassathletics.com

McDaniel College Green Terror
- *McDaniel's mascot sports a brand new look.* mcdaniel.edu

Mercer University Bears
- *Traditions.* mercer.edu

Miami Hurricanes
- Traditions. welcome.miami.edu

Michigan State Spartans
- Darden Livesay. *Ever Wonder How the Spartans Got Their Name?* pappaspost.com (April 23, 2025)
- *Michigan State Athletics History & Traditions.* msuspartans.com

Michigan Wolverines
- *Michigan vs Ohio State: The Wolverine.* bentley.umich.edu

Millikin University Big Blue
- *Big Blue Athletics History.* athletics.millikin.edu

Minnesota Golden Gophers
- Allison Daniel. *Weird Mascots in College Sports.* thetigercu.com. (Feb. 25, 2016)

Minnesota North College – Rainy River Voyageurs
- *RRCC to rebrand.* twincities.com (Feb. 6, 2025)

Mississippi Rebels
- *Before we were the Ole Miss Rebels.* oxfordeagle.com (Oct. 25, 2015)
- *Traditions.* olemisssports.com

Mississippi State Bulldogs
- Jacob Manley. *The History of the Mississippi State Cowbell.* southboundanddown.com (July 31, 2024)

Missouri Tigers
- *Truman the Tiger.* mutigers.com

Missouri-Kansas City Kangaroos
- *Traditions/History.* kcroos.com

Missouri-St. Louis Tritons
- *Meet Louie.* umsl.edu

Moody Bible Institute Archers
- *The Moody Archers Story.* moodyarchers.org

Mount Holyoke College Lyons
- *Why Lyons?* athletics.mtholyoke.edu

Murray State Racers
- *Traditions.* goracers.com

Navy Midshipmen
- *Goats and the U.S. Navy.* history.navy.mil

Nebraska Cornhuskers
- *Origin of the Cornhusker Nickname.* huskers.com (July 24, 2017)

Nevada Wolf Pack
- *Wolf Pack Traditions.* nevadawolfpack.com

New Jersey City University Gothic Knights
- *James Betelle, Where Are You?* jamesbetelle.com

New Mexico Lobos
- *Lobo Nickname.* golobos.com

New School of Florida Mighty Banyans
- Curt Anderson. *Conservative trustees choose 'Mighty Banyans' for Florida college mascot.* Associated Press. (June 1, 2023)

North Carolina State Wolfpack
- *The Origin of the 'Wolfpack'* gopack.com
- *Why Is NC State Called the Wolfpack?* ncsu.edu

North Carolina Tar Heels
- *Traditions – Mascot.* goheels.com
- *Why We're All Called Tar Heels.* alumni.unc.edu

North Carolina Wesleyan University Battling Bishops
- *We are Battling Bishops.* ncwu.edu

North Dakota Fighting Hawks
- Aliah Williamson. *University of North Dakota changes controversial mascot name.* (Nov. 19, 2015) wtkr.com
- *Fighting Hawks picked as new University of North Dakota nickname.* Associated Press. (Nov. 18, 2015)

North Florida Ospreys
- Gary Warner. *How the Osprey Became UNF's Mascot.* libguides.unf.edu

North Greenville Trailblazers
- Marty O'Gwynn. *North Greenville Seeks to Honor History, Blaze Trail With New Mascot.* ngu.edu (April 30, 2024)

North Texas Mean Green
- Randy Cummings. *The Origin of the Mean Green.* meangreensports.com

Northwest Nazarene University Nighthawks
- *Meet Our Mascot.* nnu.edu

Northwestern State University
- *Vic the Demon.* nsutraditions.com

Northwestern Wildcats
- *History of Northwestern Trademarks.* northwestern.edu

Notre Dame Fighting Irish
- Matt Keough. *The history of the University of Notre Dame's famed moniker and mascot the Fighting Irish leprechaun.* irishcentral.com. (April 1, 2013)
- *The Fighting Irish.* fightingirish.com

Oberlin College Yeomen
- *Why Yeomen?* goyeo.com

Oglethorpe University Stormy Petrels
- *Our Mascot: The Stormy Petrel.* gopetrels.com

Ohio State Buckeyes
- Joe Grobeck. *Ohio State's "Dotting the I": The Iconic 85-Year-Old Band Tradition.* fanbuzz.com (Sept. 15, 2021)
- *What Is a Buckeye?* ohiostatebuckeyes.com

Oklahoma Sooners
- *OU Mascots.* soonersports.com. (Oct. 24, 2023)
- *What is a Sooner?* soonersports.com. (May 20, 2013)

Oklahoma State Cowboys
- *America's favorite mascot.* go.okstate.edu

Olivet College Comets
- Emily Cusack. *Before the Comets were Comets.* occcho.com. (Feb. 14, 2016)

Oregon Ducks
- Ryan Clarke. *It's 'The Duck,' not 'Puddles': A definitive history of the Oregon mascot.* oregonlive.com. (Oct. 23, 2024)
- *The Oregon Duck.* goducks.com

Penn Quakers
- Richard Zhuang. *The essential Penn traditions to know, from toast throwing to Spring Fling.* thedp.com. (Aug. 19, 2024)

Penn State Nittany Lions
- *The origin of the Nittany Lion.* psu.edu

Pennsylvania Western University California Vulcans
- *Meet Our Mascot, Blaze.* pennwest.edu

Pikes Peak College Aardvarks
- *Timeline.* pikespeak.edu

Pittsburg State Gorillas
- *Evolution of the Gorillas.* pittstategorillas.com

Princeton Tigers
- *The Tiger.* princetoniana.princeton.edu

Providence Christian College Sea Beggars
- *About – Sea Beggars.* providencecc.edu

Purdue Boilermakers
- *Boilermaker name.* purdue-traditions.weebly.com

Purdue-Fort Wayne Mastodons
- *Mastodon History, Spirit, and Traditions.* pfw.edu

Quinsigamond Community College Wyverns
- *Wyvern Wishes a Successful Spring Semester During First Days of Class.* qcc.edu. (Jan. 30, 2025)

Rhode Island School of Design Nads
- Brain VanHooker. *The Story of Scrotie.* melmagazine.com

Richmond Spiders
- *Why We're "Spiders".* richmondspiders.com

River Parishes Community College Rougarous
- *History of the Rougarou: Louisiana's Werewolf.* pelicanstateofmind.com

Robert Morris Colonials
- Ehsan Kassim. *Where is Robert Morris located?* sports.yahoo.com. (March 21, 2025)

Rocky Mountain College Battlin' Bears
- *Rocky Football History.* gobattlinbears.com

Rollins College Tars
- Bobby Davis. *What's a Tar?* rollins.edu (Aug. 17, 2015)

Rowan University Profs
- Heath Bernstein. *What's a Prof? Why I think it is time to change our name.* thewhitonline.com (Sept. 27, 2023)

Saint Louis University Billikens
- *SLU's Mascot: The Billiken.* slu.edu

Saint Mary-of-the-Woods Pomeroys
- *What is a Pomeroy?* smwcathletics.com

Sam Houston State Bearkats
- *The Bearkat Mascot.* shsu.edu

Samford Bulldogs
- *Bulldog Club.* samfordsports.com

Santa Clara Broncos
- Sahale Greenwood. *Who Are We, Broncos?* magazine.scu.edu (March 6, 2020)

Santa Monica Corsairs
- *What is a "Corsair"? The secret behind the name.* thecorsaironline.com

Scottsdale Fighting Artichokes
- Mark Nothaft. *Is Scottsdale Community College's mascot really an artichoke?* azcentral.com. (Oct. 4, 2016)

SMU Mustangs
- *Peruna.* smu.edu

Snead Community College Parsons
- *Fan Zone.* sneadathletics.com

South Carolina Gamecocks
- Chris Horn. *Why are we Gamecocks?* sc.edu (Feb. 4, 2020)
- Ryan McGee. *The Ballad of Sir Big Spur: South Carolina's strange-but-true tale of a live mascot handler feud.* espn.com. (Sept 16, 2022)

South Dakota State Jackrabbits
- *Traditions.* gojacks.com

Southern New Hampshire University Penmen
- *We Are Penmen.* campus.snhu.edu

Southern University Jaguars
- Thomas Aiello. *Bayou Classic: The Grambling-Southern Football Rivalry.* thomasaiellobooks.com.

Southwestern College Moundbuilders
- *Do you know the history of the Mound?* ps.sckans.edu

St. Ignatius Gray Fog
- *What's a Don?* usfca.edu

St. Josephs Hawks
- Andrew Grath. *How does the St. Joe's Hawk mascot flap his wings 3,500 times a game? "It's my love of St. Joe's"* cbsnews.com (Jan. 21, 2025)

Stanford Cardinal
- *On Campus.* gostanford.com (April 17, 2013)
- Paridhi Bhatia. *The Stanford Tree turns over a new leaf.* stanforddaily.com (May 7, 2024)

Stetson Hatters
- *Spirit and Traditions.* gohatters.com

Stevens Institute of Technology Ducks
- *Attila the Duck Profile.* stevensducks.com

SUNY Potsdam Bears
- *Mascot History.* potsdam.edu

Syracuse Orange
- *The Syracuse Orange.* cuse.com

Taylor University Trojans
- Jeff Esienberg. *The most wonderful time of the year*. taylortrojans.com

TCU Horned Frogs
- David Stein. *What is a Horned Frog, anyway?* admissions.tcu.edu. (July 8, 2019)

Tennessee Volunteers
- Ann Topovich. *Volunteer State*. tennesseeencyclopedia.net
- Keenan Thomas. *Why are Davy Crockett and Smokey both University of Tennessee mascots?* Knoxville News Sentinel. (March 22, 2024)

Texas A&M Aggies
- *12th Man*. tamu.edu
- *Reveille*. tamu.edu

Texas A&M-Kingsville Javelinas
- *What is a Javelina?* tamuk.edu

Texas Longhorns
- *The Truth About Bevo*. texasexes.org
- *Why are we Longhorns?* jimnicar.com

Texas Tech Red Raiders
- Brandi D. Addison. *Why do Texas Tech fans toss tortillas during games? There are a few theories*. lubbockonline.com (Aug. 27, 2024)
- *Masked Rider*. ttu.edu

Tohono O'odham Community College Jegos
- Jacelle Ramon-Sauberan. *Basketball Comes to Tohono O'odham Community College*. ictnews.org. (Sept. 23, 2011)

Toledo Rockets
- Andy Wittry. *Here's the true story about how Toledo got the nickname 'Rockets'*. ncaa.com. (Oct. 2, 2020)

Trinity Christian Trolls
- *History of the Troll*. trollsathletics.com

Trinity College Bantams
- *A Brief History*. bantamsports.com.

Trinity University Tigers
- *Trinity Before the Tigers*. spmt3314.coateslibrary.com

Troy Trojans
- *What Is a Trojan?* troytrojans.com

Truett-McConnell University Bears
- Jenny Gregory. *TMC Mascot Changes*. truett.edu. (Jan. 1, 2006)

Tufts University
- Francis Storrs. *The Great Barnum Fire: An Oral History*. tufts.edu. (Jan. 17, 2017)

Tulane Green Wave
- *History of the Green Wave*. tulanegreenwave.com (Jan. 13, 2011)

U.S. Air Force Academy Falcons
- *The Contrails: U.S. Air Force Academy Mascot*. usafa.af.mil. (Feb. 18, 2016)

U.S. Coast Guard Academy Bears
- *Objee the Bear*. uscga.edu

UC Irvine Anteaters
- Andy Wittry. *Here's the true story about how UC Irvine got the nickname 'Anteaters'*. ncaa.com. (July 7, 2022)

UC Riverside Highlanders
- *Highlander History*. studentlife.ucr.edu

UC Santa Barbera Gauchos
- John Zant. *UCSB's Forgotten Football History*. independent.com. (April 23, 2015)

UC Santa Cruz Banana Slugs
- *How the Banana Slug became UCSC's official mascot*. ucsc.edu

UCLA Bruins
- Fiona Ruane. *From 'Rags' to Bruins*. newsroom.ucla.edu (April 2, 2024)

Union College Garnet Chargers
- *Union drops Dutchmen/Dutchwomen nickname, to be known as Garnet Chargers moving forward*. uscho.com (Aug. 4, 2023)

University of Alabama in Huntsville Chargers
- Michael Napier. *The UAH Chargers Mascot*. uahchargers.com

University of Chicago Maroons
- *Maroon, Maroons, and the Phoenix*. athletics.uchicago.edu

University of Health Sciences and Pharmacy Eutectics
- *Meet Morty the Eutectic*. eutecticsports.com.

UNLV Rebels
- Michelle Rindels. *UNLV president says keep Rebel name; no Confederate roots*. Associated Press. (Nov. 30, 2015)

USC Trojans
- Andy Wittry. *How USC got the nickname Trojans.* ncaa.com. (July 8, 2022)
- *Traveler.* usctrojans.com

Utah Utes
- *What is a Ute?* utahutes.com

UTEP Miners
- *Miner Traditions.* utep.edu

Valparaiso Beacons
- *Valparaiso University Unveils New Nickname.* valpo.edu

Vanderbilt Commodores
- *History of Vanderbilt University.* vanderbilt.edu

Vassar Brewers
- David Levine. *Looking Back on the Origins of Vassar College in Poughkeepsie.* hvmag.com. (May 19, 2022)

Vermont Catamounts
- April McCullum. *The strange tale of how UVM became the Catamounts.* vermontpublic.org (Dec. 17, 2024)

Villanova Wildcats
- Brian Ewart. *Wildcats are the 4th most common Division I mascot.* vuhoops.com. (April 1, 2013)

Virginia Cavaliers
- *Traditions.* virginiasports.com

Virginia Military Institute Keydets
- *Mascot History.* vmikeydets.com

Virginia Tech Hokies
- Andy Wittry. *How Virginia Tech got the nickname 'Hokies'.* ncaa.com (Sept. 21, 2020)
- *How 'Enter Sandman' became the most electric entrance in college football.* hokiesports.com (June 27, 2024)

Wabash College Little Giants
- *Wabash Athletics History.* sports.wabash.edu

Wake Forest Demon Deacons
- Andy Wittry. *How Wake Forest got the nickname Demon Deacons.* ncaa.com (July 8, 2022)

Washburn Ichabods
- *Ichabod mascot.* washburn.edu

Washington Huskies
- *Mascot History.* gohuskies.com

Washington State Cougars
- Beanna Greene. *Mascot Mania: How the Cougars became the Cougars.* krem.com. (July 2, 2020)

Weber State Wildcats
- *History.* weber.edu

Webster University Gorloks
- *The Gorlok.* websterathletics.com

West Virginia Mountaineers
- *Traditions.* mountaineernationday.wvu.edu.

Western Carolina Catamounts
- Erik Hall. *What is a Catamount? We have your answer Western Carolina fans.* citizen-times.com. (Dec. 18, 2018)

Western Illinois Leathernecks
- *The Leatherneck Nickname.* goleathernecks.com

Western Kentucky Hilltoppers
- *Big Red.* wkusports.com

Wheaton College Lyons
- *"Y" The Lyons?* wheatoncollegelyons.com

Wichita State Shockers
- *WuShock.* goshockers.com

Williams College Ephs
- *Why Ephs, Purple, and Purple Cows?* ephsports.williams.edu

Wisconsin Badgers
- *Badger Nickname.* uwbadgers.com
- Mark Knight. *Why does Wisconsin do the Jump Around tradition?* badgerofhonor.com. (July 2, 2025)

Wyoming Cowboys
- *Cowboys.* gowyo.com.

Xavier University Musketeers
- *One For All.* goxavier.com.

Yavapai College Roughriders
- *Ruff the YC Mascot.* yc.edu.

Index

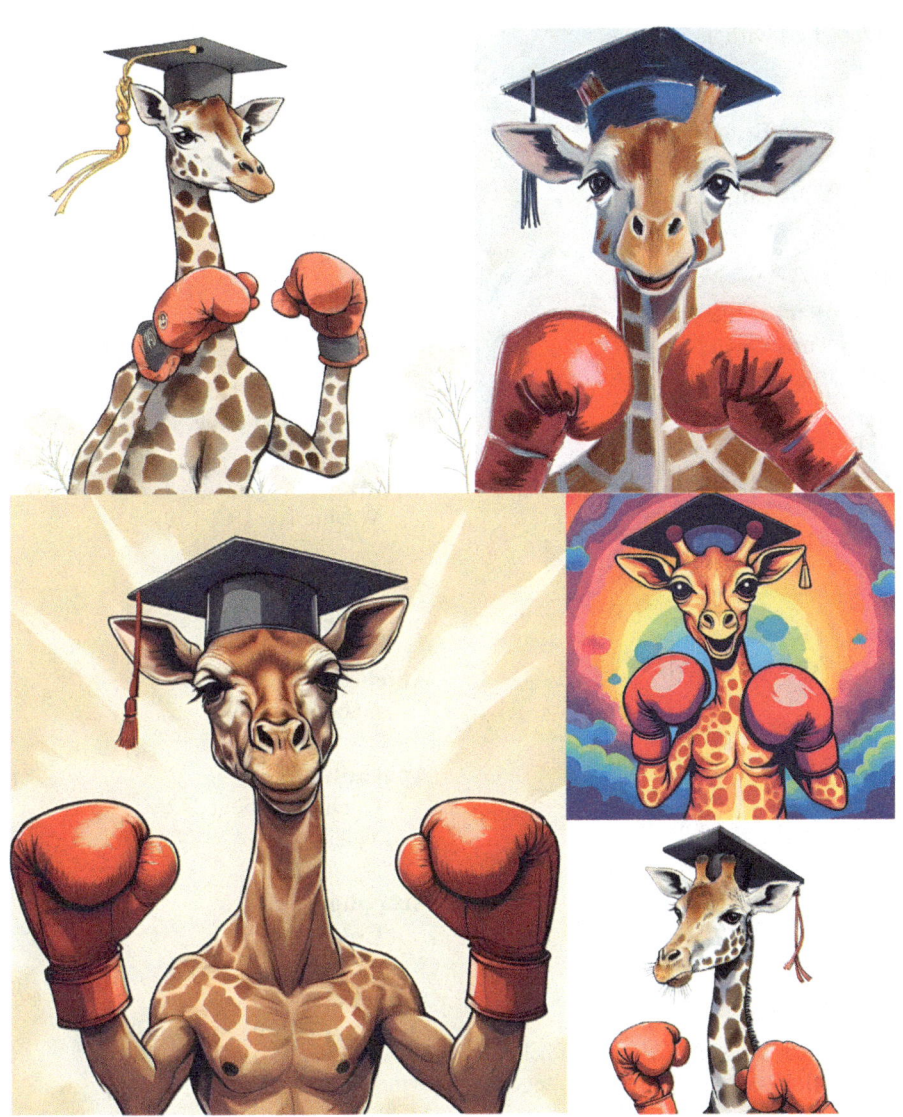

The following index includes current and past nicknames for schools. At the end is a list of the nicknames that could have been if elections or committees had gone in a different direction. Fictional teams are identified with an asterisk.

49ers
Long Beach State, 10
UNC-Charlotte, 10
Yuba College, 10

A

Aardvarks, 179
Aims CC, 11
Pikes Peak State, 10

Abejas
Universidad de Guanajuato, 74

Anteaters
UC Irvine, 11

Aggie Rams
Colorado A&M, 98

Aggies, 52
Arkansas State, 52, 90
Cameron University, 51
Colorado A&M, 98
Colorado State, 52
Connecticut, 52
Delaware Valley, 51
Doña Ana CC, 51
Kansas State, 52
Massachusetts, 52
Massachusetts Agricultural, 131
Michigan Agricultural College, 133
Michigan State, 52
Mississippi State, 52
Nebraska College of Tech Agriculture, 51
New Mexico State, 51, 106, 170
North Carolina A&T State, 51
North Carolina State, 52, 149
Oklahoma A&M, 155
Oklahoma Panhandle State, 51
Oklahoma State, 52
Oregon State, 52
Rhode Island, 52
Second District Agricultural School, 47
Texas A&M, 5, 51, 96, 106, 127, 165, 168-171
UC Davis, 51, 126
Utah State, 51, 170
Washington State, 175

Alphas
Washtenaw CC, 150

AmCats
Anna Maria College, 59

Antelopes
Nebraska, 139

Apaches
Cochise College, 72
Tyler JC, 72

Arapahoes
Colorado, 98

Archers
Moody Bible Institute, 115
St. Louis CC, 61

Argonauts, 71

Armadillos
Texas State*, 65

Arrows
Ursuline, 150

Artichokes
Scottsdale CC, 22

Athenas
Claremont-Mudd-Scripps, 71

Athenians
Mount St. Mary's, 71

Atlanteans
Atlantis University, 71

Atoms
Adams*, 65

Auggies
Augsburg University, 77

Avenging Angels
Meredith College, 50

Aviators
Arkansas State-Newport, 75

Axemen
Acadia University, 73

Aztecs
Pima CC, 72
San Diego State, 72, 171

B

Badgers
Wisconsin, 171, 178

Bald Eagles
Lock Haven, 63

Balls
Rhode Island School of Design, 160

Banana Slugs
UC Santa Cruz, 4, 11-12

Bandits
Clatsop CC, 70, 150

Bantams
Idaho Tech, 110
Trinity, 100

Baptists
Mercer, 105

Barons
Brewton-Parker Christian, 108
Rowan College, 141-142

Battlin' Bears
Rocky Mountain College, 139

Battling Bishops
North Carolina Wesleyan, 59, 147
Ohio Wesleyan, 59

Bayhawks
Bristol CC, 67

Beach
Long Beach State, 10

Beacons
Valparaiso, 117

Bearcats, 55
Cincinnati, 56, 171
Northwest Missouri, 107

Bearkats
Sam Houston State, 53, 55, 166

Bears, 6, 79
Athens State, 86
Baylor, 96, 165, 170
Brown University, 160
Mercer, 105
Morgan State, 96
Rocky Mountain College, 139
SUNY-Potsdam, 144
Truett-McConnell, 108
U.S. Coast Guard Academy, 99

Beavers
Bemidji State, 134
Oregon State, 38, 171

Bees, 54

Bengals
Idaho State, 106, 110

Bennies
College of Saint Benedict, 77

Big Blue
Millikin University, 111

Big Green
Dartmouth, 59, 106, 141
Marshall, 177

Big Horns
Colorado, 98
Eastern Colorado*, 65

Big Red
Cornell, 106, 143

Bigfoot
CC of Spokane, 41

Billikens
Saint Louis University, 12-13, 61

Bison
Howard, 97

Bisons
Harding University, 90-91

Black Bears
Maine, 126, 128-129

Black Flies
College of the Atlantic, 128

Black Hawks
Black River Tech, 67

Black Knights
Army, 107, 143, 171

Black Widow Spiders
North Greenville, 161

Blackhawks
Southeastern CC, 67

Blazers
Alabama-Birmingham, 170

Bleu Devils
Dillard University, 53

Bloodhounds
John Jay College, 62

Blue
Wellesley, 60

Blue Demons
DePaul, 113-114

Blue Devils, 6, 57
Duke, 57
Trinity, 19

Blue Hawks
Dickinson State, 67, 152

Blue Hens
Delaware, 26, 100

Blue Hose
Presbyterian College, 50, 150

Blue Raiders
Middle Tennessee State, 170

Blue Storm
Southwestern Illinois, 80

Blueboys
Illinois College, 115

BlueWaves
Florida State College, 150

Blugolds
Wisconsin-Eau Claire, 150

Bobcats
Montana State, 170
Ohio University, 107

Boilermakers
Purdue, 13, 96, 171

Bold
Toronto Metro University, 73

Boll Weevils
Arkansas-Monticello, 15
Enterprise State CC, 14-15

Bombers
Ithaca, 144

Bonnies
St. Bonaventure, 107

Border Collies
Spartanburg, 62

Boxers
Black Hawk, 72

Braves
Albion College, 68
Alcorn State, 97, 171
Bradley, 106, 126
North Carolina-Pembroke, 72
Washington State, 175

'Breds
Murray State, 123

Brewers
  Vassar College, 74, 145
  Williamsburg Tech, 74
Bridges
  Brooklyn College, 143
Britons
  Albion College, 68, 106, 133
Broncbusters
  Garden City CC, 52
Bronchos
  Central Oklahoma, 53
Broncos
  Santa Clara, 94
Bruins
  California Berkeley, 57
  UCLA, 57, 107
Buccaneers, 70
Buckeyes
  Ohio State, 5, 15-16, 154, 171
Buffaloes
  Colorado, 98, 171
Bugeaters
  Nebraska, 139
Builders
  Apprentice School, 174
Bulldogs, 58, 62, 79
  Arizona State, 88
  Brooklyn College, 143
  Butler, 58
  Cumberland, 163
  Fresno State, 127, 171
  Georgia, 58, 97, 104-105, 108, 127
  Louisiana Tech, 34
  Minnesota-Duluth, 170
  Mississippi State, 135-136, 170
  Northern Colorado, 97
  Samford, 84
  South Carolina State, 96
  SW Louisiana Institute, 124
  Troy, 87
  Yale, 6, 58, 126, 171
Bullets
  Gettysburg, 96, 160
Bulls
  Buffalo, 97
  South Florida, 96
Burros Blancas
  Instituto Politécnico Nacional, 74
Bushmen
  Southern University, 124

C

Cadets
  Oklahoma Military Academy, 156
Caimans
  Hostos College, 77
Camels
  Campbell, 148
  Connecticut College, 99-100

Cannoneers
Jefferson CC, 60
Pratt Institute, 60

Captains
Christopher Newport University, 74

Cardinal
Stanford, 16, 94, 170

Cardinals, 56
Arkansas, 39
Ball State, 106, 118, 170
Louisville, 122-123, 171

Cascades
Fraser Valley, 73

Catamounts, 61
Vermont, 173
Western Carolina, 147

Catawba Indians
Catawba College, 72, 148-149

Catholics
Notre Dame, 24

Cats
Southern University, 124

Cavaliers, 60
Virginia, 173-174

Cayugas
Ithaca, 144

Celtics
Carlow University, 68

Celts
St. Thomas, 68

Centurions
Bucks County, 61
Montcalm, 61

Chanticleers
Coastal Carolina, 16

Chargers
Hillsdale, 132
University of Alabama in Huntsville, 85

Chiefs
Springfield College, 131
Washington State, 175
Waubonsee, 72

Chippewas
Central Michigan, 72, 126

Choctaws
Mississippi College, 72

Chokers
Gray Harbor, 77, 176

CityHawks
CC of Denver, 67

Claim Jumpers
Columbia College, 17

Cliffdwellers
Columbia (OR), 157

Cobbers
Concordia College, 18

Cobras, 54, 77

Collegians
Athens College, 86

Colonels
Centre College, 123-124

Colonials
Robert Morris, 159

Colts
Richmond, 175

Comets
Capital University, 154
College of the Mainland, 168
Olivet College, 134

Commodores
Gulf Coast State, 102
Vanderbilt, 97, 102, 106, 163

Condors
Oxnard, 56

Congregationalists
Olivet College, 134

Continentals
Hamilton, 107

Corncobs
Concordia College, 18

Cornhuskers
Nebraska, 52, 139

Correcaminos
Universidad Autónoma de Tamaulipas, 74

Corsairs
College of the Redwoods, 93
Santa Monica, 92-93

Cotton Blossoms
Arkansas-Monticello, 15, 76

Cougars, 5, 61, 64, 79
Brigham Young, 171
Harrison*, 65
Houston, 61, 167-168, 170
Misercordia, 126
Washington State, 61, 170, 175

Cowboys, 52
Oklahoma State, 155, 170
Wyoming, 97, 107, 179

Coyotes
Compton College, 93

Cranes
Port Chester University*, 65

Crimson
Harvard, 6, 107, 171

Crimson Bulldogs
Howard College, 84

Crimson Comets
Olivet College, 134

Crimson Hawks
Indiana University (PA), 67

Crimson Pride
Indiana-Columbus, 60

196

Crimson Tide
Alabama, 4, 18-19, 84-85, 87, 97, 126, 171

Crimson Storm
Southern Nazarene, 80

Crusaders
Capital University, 154
Holy Cross, 96, 106
North Greenville, 161
Northwest Nazarene, 109-110
Valparaiso, 117

Crush
Clovis CC, 150

Cubs
UCLA, 57

Cyclones, 80
Iowa State, 119, 171

D

Dales
Hillsdale, 132

Deans
Hawaii, 38

Delta Devils
Mississippi Valley State, 97, 106

Delta Dragons
East Arkansas, 89

Demon Deacons
Wake Forest, 19

Demons
Northwestern State, 125

Desert Warriors
Imperial Valley, 61

Diamond Danes
Truett-McConnell, 108

Diplomats
Franklin & Marshall College, 75, 157-158

Dirtbags
Long Beach State, 20

Dolphins, 70
Western University*, 65

Dons
San Francisco, 95

Drovers
Scottsdale CC, 22
University of Science and Arts of Oklahoma, 156

Ducks
Oregon, 20-21, 156, 171
Stevens Institute, 21

Duhawks
Loras College, 67, 150

Dukes
James Madison, 174

Dustdevils
Texas A&M International, 80

Dutch
Central College, 68

Dutchmen
Union College, 144

Dutchwomen
Union College, 144

E

Eagle Owls
Jacksonville State, 26

Eagles, 7, 56, 59, 63, 79
Cadwallader University*, 65
Georgia Southern, 126, 171
North Carolina Central, 96
North Texas, 37

Engineers
Massachusetts Institute of
Technology, 106, 127

Ephs
Williams College, 21, 107

Eutectics
UHSP, 22

Excalibur
Trent University, 73

Explorers
La Salle University, 159

F

Falcons, 56, 79
Hillman College*, 65
U.S. Air Force Academy, 95

Farmers, 51
Arkansas State, 90
North Carolina State, 149
Washington State, 175

Fightin' Christians
Elon College, 148

Fightin' Engineers
Rose-Hulman, 66

Fighting Artichokes
Scottsdale CC, 22

Fighting Bees
St. Ambrose, 50-51

Fighting Cacti
Copper Mountain, 66

Fighting Camels
Campbell, 5, 66, 97, 126, 148

Fighting Cephalopods
Miskatonic*, 65

Fighting Comets
College of the Mainland, 168

Fighting Ducks
College of the Mainland, 56, 168

Fighting Geese
Gainesville State, 109

Fighting Hawks
North Dakota, 67, 152

Fighting Illini
Illinois, 24, 107, 171

Fighting Indians
Haskell Indian Nations, 72

Fighting Irish
Notre Dame, 24, 116

Fighting Lords
Kenyon College, 154-155

Fighting Lutherans
Capital University, 154

Fighting Muskies
Muskingum College, 66

Fighting Okra
Delta State, 23

Fighting Owls
Harford, 66

Fighting Pickles
North Carolina School of the Arts, 23

Fighting Pinecones
Redwood State*, 65

Fighting Presbyterians
Alma College, 132

Fighting Saints
Carroll College, 59
St. Francis, 59

Fighting Scots, 68

Fighting Sioux
North Dakota, 152

Fighting Spirits
Wisconsin-Baraboo Sauk County, 66

Fighting Squirrels
Mary Baldwin University, 55, 126, 150

Fillies
Panola College, 64, 150

Fire
Southeastern, 66

Fire Ants
South Carolina-Sumter, 55

Firehawks
Tennessee Southern, 56, 66, 67

Firestorm
Arizona Christian, 66, 150

Flames, 66

Flyers
Dayton, 67
Lewis University, 67
Sandhills CC, 67

Flying Dutchmen
Hope College, 67
Lebanon Valley, 67, 158-159

Flying Fleet
Erskine College, 161-162

Flying Queens
Wayland Baptist, 67, 150

Flying Squadron
Virginia Military Institute, 174

Flying Tigers
SOWELA Tech, 64

Fords
Haverford College, 150

Foresters, 77
Huntington, 117

Friars
Providence, 107
Santa Clara, 94

Frogs
Quinebaug Valley CC, 53

Frontiersmen
Colorado, 98

G

Gaels
Iona, 68
St. Mary's, 68

Gamecocks
Jacksonville State, 26, 96
South Carolina, 16, 25-26, 161

Garnet
Swarthmore College, 150

Garnet Chargers
Union College, 59, 144

Gansos Salvajes
Universidad Autónoma de Guadalajara, 74

Gators, 69, 77, 97
Allegheny, 126
Brazosport College, 179
Florida, 69, 126

Gauchos
UC Santa Barbara, 93-94, 106

Geckos
GateWay, 77

Generals
LSU-Alexandria, 125

Gentlemen
Centenary, 125

Geoducks
Evergreen State, 27

Giants
Keystone College, 157

Gila Monsters
Eastern Arizona, 77

Gladiators
Chabot College, 60

Gobblers
Virginia Tech, 30

Gold Nuggets
Xavier University of Louisiana, 60, 150

Gold Rush
Xavier University of Louisiana, 60

Golden Bears, 60
Alberta, 73
California Berkeley, 57, 170
Kutztown, 126

Golden Bulls
Johnson C. Smith, 60

Golden Eagles, 60, 63
John Brown University, 90
Marquette, 107
Tennessee Tech, 107

Golden Falcons
Felician University, 60, 142

Golden Flashes
Kent State, 60, 153

Golden Flyers
Nazareth College, 60

Golden Gophers
Minnesota, 55, 60, 134-135, 171

Golden Griffins
Canisus, 60

Golden Grizzlies
Oakland University, 60

Golden Gusties
Gustavus Adolphus, 59, 60, 106

Golden Hurricane
Tulsa, 60, 80

Golden Knights, 60

Golden Lions, 60
Arkansas-Pine Bluff, 96

Golden Norsemen
Northeastern Oklahoma A&M, 60, 68, 150

Golden Panthers
Florida International, 103

Golden Rams, 60

Golden Seals, 60

Golden Suns
Sheldon Jackson College, 88

Golden Tigers, 60

Golden Tornadoes
Geneva College, 60, 80

Golden Wolves
Alvernia University, 60

Gophers
Minnesota, 134-135

Gorillas
Arkansas State, 90
Pittsburg State, 27-28

Gorlocks
Webster University, 138

Gothic Knights
New Jersey City University, 141

Governors
Austin Peay, 96, 164

Grandees
Loyola University, 112

Gray Fog
St. Ignatius, 95

Great Danes
Albany, 62
Truett-McConnell, 108

Green Jays
Jackson State CC, 150

Green Terror
McDaniel College, 60, 129, 179

Green Wave
Tulane, 124

Greenbacks
Tulane, 124

Gremlins
Greenville College, 115

Greyhounds, 62

Griffins, 53
Westminster College, 172

Griffons
Missouri Western State, 53

Grizzlies
Colorado, 98
Montana, 57, 170
UCLA, 57

Gryphons
Sarah Lawrence, 53

Gussies
Pittsburg State, 28

Gymnasts
Springfield College, 131

Gyrenes
Ave Maria University, 104

H

Hardrockers
South Dakota School of Mines and Technology, 163, 170

Harriers
Furman, 161
Miami-Hamilton, 56

Harvesters
Dallas Eastfield, 52

Hatters
Stetson, 28-29

Hawkeyes
Iowa, 29, 119, 171

Hawks, 56, 67, 79
Hudson*, 65
Saint Joseph's, 158

Hayseeds
Washington State, 175

Highlanders, 68
UC Riverside, 92

Hillcats
Rogers State, 156

Hilltoppers
Brown University, 160
Western Kentucky, 123, 170

Hornets
Furman 161
Kalamazoo, 106

Hokams
Mesa CC, 89

Hokies
Virginia Tech, 29-30, 173

Hoos
Virginia, 173-174

Hoosieroons
Ball State, 118

Hoosiers
Indiana, 30, 171

Hooters
Grand Lakes University*, 65

Horned Frogs
TCU, 5, 31-32, 170

Hornets
Alabama State, 97
Campbell, 148

Hounds
Dominican University of California, 38

Hoyas
Georgetown, 176

Human Beings
Greendale CC*, 65

Humpback Whales
Alaska Southeast, 55

Hurricanes, 80
Miami, 103

Huskies, 62
Hudson*, 65
Michigan Tech, 126
Northeastern, 127
Northern Illinois, 170
St. Cloud State, 170
Washington, 170, 176

Hustlin' Owls
Oregon Institute of Technology, 55

Hylanders
UC Riverside, 92

I

IceHawks
Lake Superior, 56, 67

Ichabods
Washburn University, 32

Indians
Arkansas State, 90
Catawba College, 148-149
Chipola College, 72
Itawamba CC, 72

Marshall, 177
McCook CC, 72
South Carolina-Salkehatchie, 72
Stanford, 16
Washington State, 175

Inferno
Alverno, 66

Iron Horses
Arkansas Hope-Texarkana, 64

Islanders
Texas A&M-Corpus Christi, 150

Itamitas
Instituto Tecnológico Autónomo de México, 74

J

Jackrabbits
South Dakota State, 55, 107, 162

Jaguar Cats
Southern University, 124

Jaguars
South Carolina College, 25
Southern University, 96, 124, 126, 170

Jaspers
Manhattan College, 146

Javelinas
Texas A&M-Kingsville, 127, 169

Jayhawks
Kansas, 33, 67, 170-171

Jazz Birds
Florida A&M, 101

Jazz Cats
Berklee College of Music, 127

Jegos
Tohono O'odham CC, 89

Jennies
Central Missouri, 63, 137

Jersey Blues
Brookdale CC, 150

Judges
Brandeis, 130

Jumbos
Tufts, 33-34, 107

K

Kangaroos, 54
Austin College, 167
Missouri-Kansas City, 137

Kats
Erie CC, 150

Keelhaulers
Cal Poly Maritime, 34

Keydets
Virginia Military Institute, 174

Kickin' Danes
Truett-McConnell, 108

Kingsmen
Brooklyn College, 143

Knights, 60, 79
    Carleton College, 170
    Central Florida, 127

Koalas
    Columbia College, 150

Kohawks
    Coe College, 67

Kougars
    Kishwaukee, 64

Kraken
    Cateret CC, 71

L

Ladies
    Centenary, 125

Lady Techsters
    Louisiana Tech, 34

Lakehawks
    Lake-Sumter State, 67

Lancers, 60

Larks
    Hesston, 150

Lasers
    Lasell, 150

Lazers
    Onondaga, 150

Leathernecks
    Western Illinois, 115

Leopards
    Lafayette College, 171

Lightning
    Goldey-Beacom, 101

Lions, 64, 79
    Columbia University, 145-146
    Southeastern Louisiana, 97

Little Giants
    Wabash College, 35

Lizards
    Hostos College, 77

Lobos
    New Mexico, 142

Loggers, 77

Longhorns
    Texas, 5, 35, 107, 126, 168-169, 171

Lopers
    Nebraska-Kearney, 139

Lord Jeffs
    Amherst, 130

Lords
    Kenyon College, 154-155

Loros
    Universidad de Colima, 73

Lumberjacks, 77

Lyons
Mount Holyoke College, 35
Wheaton College, 35

M

Maccabees
Yeshiva University, 60

Magicians
LeMoyne-Owen, 75

Mainland Comets
College of the Mainland, 168

Mammoths
Amherst, 130-131

Manatees
State of College Manatee-Sarasota, 70

Maple Leafs
Goshen College, 76

Marauders
Central State, 153-154

Marauding Eagles
Marycrest International, 120

Marlins
Virginia Wesleyan, 70

Maroon and Gold
Loyola University, 112

Maroons
Chicago, 81, 112-113
Southern Illinois, 114
Springfield College, 131

Mastodons
Purdue-Fort Wayne, 118

Mauve
Kenyon College, 154-155

Mavericks
Minnesota State, 97, 127

Mean Green
North Texas, 37

Mechanics
Williams College of Trade, 75

Men in Red
Fairfield, 100

Methodists
Southwestern College, 121

Michaelmen
Saint Michael's College, 173

Midshipmen
Navy, 106, 129, 143, 171

Mighty Banyans
New College of Florida, 76, 102-103

Mighty Macs
Immaculate University, 50, 77

Mighty Moose Herd
Wossamatta U*, 37-38

Mighty Oaks, 76
BYU-Idaho, 110-111

Miners
UTEP, 127, 166, 170

Minutemen
Massachusetts, 131-132

Mission Lads
Santa Clara, 94

Missionites
Santa Clara, 94

Moccasins
Florida Southern, 77

Mocs
Tennessee-Chattanooga, 151

Moles
Nazareth College, 134

Mongols
Faber College*, 65

Monks
Saint Joseph's College of Maine, 75

Moonshiners
North Greenville, 161

Moundbuilders
Southwestern College, 121

Mountain Hawks
Lehigh, 67, 107, 171

Mountain Lions, 61

Mountaineers
Appalachian State, 106, 127
North Greenville, 161
Truett-McConnell, 108
West Virginia, 170, 176-177

Mud Dogs
South Central Louisiana State*, 65

Mules
Central Missouri, 106, 137
Colby College, 128

Muleriders
Southern Arkansas, 91
Third District Agricultural School, 91

Musketeers
Xavier University, 152-153

Muskies
Lakeland College, 178

Mustangs, 63
Cal Poly, 107
SMU, 107, 167, 170

Mystics
Bismarck, 151

N

Nads
Rhode Island School of Design, 160

Nanooks
Alaska-Fairbanks, 88

Narwhals
The New School, 70, 126

Navigators
Goodwin University, 74

Nebraskans
Nebraska, 139

Nevoians
Franklin & Marshall, 157-158

Night Hawks
Thomas University, 67

Nighthawks, 67
North Georgia, 109
Northwest Nazarene, 107, 109-110

Nittany Lions
Penn State, 37-38

Nittany Tide
Springfield University*, 65

Nor'easters
University of New England, 80

Normal Lights
Dickinson State, 152

Normals
Central Missouri State, 137
Sam Houston State, 166

Norse, 68

Norsemen
North Hennepen, 68

Northern Lights
Montana State-Northern, 138

Null Set
New College of Florida, 102

O

Oaks, 76

Ocelots
Schoolcraft College, 64

Old Gold Knights
Nebraska, 139

Old Liners
Maryland, 130

Oles
St. Olaf, 78, 107, 170

Ooks
Northern Alberta Institute of Technology, 73

Orange
Syracuse, 59, 145

Orcas
Whatcom CC, 70

Orediggers
Colorado School of Mines, 95

Ospreys
North Florida, 102

Owls, 56
Charlotte College, 10
Florida Atlantic - 96
Kennesaw State, 127
Kenyon College, 154-155
Temple, 96, 127
Rice, 170

P

Paladins
  Furman, 60, 161

Palominos
  Laredo College, 63
  Palo Alto, 63

Pandas
  Alberta, 73

Panthers, 61, 64, 79
  Florida International, 103
  Georgia State, 171
  Greenville University, 115
  Pittsburgh, 170
  Prairie View A&M, 96

Parsons
  Snead State, 59

Peacocks
  Upper Iowa, 120

Penguins
  Dominican University of
    California, 38
  Penbrook*, 65
  Youngstown State, 38

Penmen
  Southern New Hampshire, 141

Phoenix
  Cumberland, 163
  Elon College, 96, 148

Pilgrims
  New England College, 68

Pilots
  Portland, 157

Pioneers, 79
  Evansville, 116
  Kenyon College, 154-155

Pipers
  Hamline University, 135

Piranhas
  Université du Québec ETS, 73

Pirates, 70
  East Carolina, 96, 127
  Hampton, 96

Poets
  Whittier College, 95

Pointers
  Wisconsin-Stevens Point, 127

Polar Bears, 54
  Bowdoin College, 128
  Ohio Northern, 97
  Potsdam State, 144

Pomeroys
  Saint Mary-of-the-Woods
    College, 116

Ponies
  Panola College, 63

Potato Diggers
  Washington State, 175

Prairie Fire
  Knox College, 113

Praying Colonels
Centre College, 123-124

Preachers
Northwest Nazarene, 109-110
Southwestern College, 121

Presidents
Washington & Jefferson College, 75, 151

Pricks
Rhode Island School of Design, 160

Pride
Clarke, 126
Springfield College, 131

Profs
Rowan University, 142

Pronghorns
Gilette College, 179

Prunepickers
Santa Clara, 94

Pueo
Hawaii-West Oahu, 109

Pumas, 61

Puritans
Brown University, 160

Purple
Kenyon College, 154-155

Purple Aces
Evansville, 60, 116

Purple Eagles
Niagara, 63

Purple Hurricanes
Furman, 161

Purple Knights
Saint Michael's College, 173

Purple Paladins
Furman, 161

Purps
Westminster College, 172

Q

Quakers, 68
Pennsylvania, 157

R

Racers
Murray State, 63, 123, 126

Racquetters
Potsdam State, 144

Ragin' Cajuns
Louisiana-Lafayette, 68, 97, 124

Raging Cajuns
Southwestern Louisiana, 124

Raiders, 70
Colgate, 106
Gaston College, 147

Railsplitters
Lincoln Memorial University, 163-164

Rainbows
Hawaii, 38

Rainbow Wahine
Hawaii, 39

Rainbow Warriors
Hawaii, 38

Rambelles
Angelo State, 151

Ramblers
Loyola University, 112
Notre Dame, 24

Rams, 79
Colorado A&M, 98-99
Colorado State, 98-99, 170

Rattlers, 77
Florida A&M, 96, 101, 127

Rattlesnake Boys
Nebraska, 139

Razorbacks
Arkansas, 39

Rebels
Gaston College, 147
Mississippi, 97, 135-136, 170-171
Nevada-Las Vegas, 97, 140

Red and Black
Louisville, 122-123

Red Flash
Saint Francis, 60

Red Hawks, 7, 67

Red Jackets
Henderson College, 91

Red Raiders
Texas Tech, 96, 165-166

Red Storm
St. John's, 80

Red Terrors
North Carolina State, 149

Red Wave
Troy, 87

Red Wolves
Arkansas State, 90, 97, 171

Reddies
Henderson State, 47, 91

RedHawks 7, 67
IU-Northwest, 53

Redhawks, 7

Redmen
Massachusetts, 131

RedStorm
Rio Grande, 53, 80

Redwoods
College of the Redwoods, 93

Reivers
Iowa Western, 120

Renegades
Bakersfield, 70
Columbia College, 70
Ohlone, 70

Retrievers
Maryland-Baltimore County, 62, 127

Revolutionaries
George Washington, 61

Rhinos
Gaston College, 147

Ridge Runners
Phillips CC, 89

River Bandits
Arkansas-Batesville, 70

River Hawks, 67

River Otters
Great Falls College, 138

Riverbats
Austin CC, 127, 151

RiverHawks, 67

Riverhawks, 67

Rivermen
Missouri-St. Louis, 138

Riverwomen
Missouri-St. Louis, 138

Roadrunners
Santa Barbara State, 93

Rockets
Toledo, 153

Rougarous
River Parishes CC, 40-41

Rough Riders
Luna CC, 143

Roughriders
Yavapai College, 89

Royal Crusaders
Crown College, 59

Runnin' Bulldogs
Gardner-Webb, 62

Runnin' Lopes
Lamar CC, 98

Runnin' Rebels
Nevada-Las Vegas, 140

Running Eagles
Life University, 63

Rustlers
Central Wyoming, 70
Golden West, 70

S

Sabercats
Marantha Baptist, 64

Sage Hens
Nevada-Reno, 140

Sage Warriors
Nevada-Reno, 140

Sagebrushers
Nevada-Reno, 140

Sagehens
Pomona-Pitzer, 7

Sailfish
Palm Beach Atlantic, 70

Saints, 79

Salukis
Southern Illinois, 62, 114-115, 126

Samsons
Gogebic CC, 132

Sand Sharks
South Carolina-Beaufort, 50

Sandwiches
South Harmon Institute of Technology*, 65

Sasquatch
CC of Spokane, 41

Savage Storm
Southeastern Oklahoma State, 80

Savages
Dickinson State, 152

Saxons
Alfred, 68, 107

Scarlet Hawks
Illinois Institute of Technology, 67

Scarlet Knights
Rutgers, 141

Scarlet Raiders
Rutgers-Newark, 141

Scarlet Raptors
Rutgers-Camden, 141

Scorpions
Nevada State, 140

Scots, 68
Alma College, 132

Screaming Eagles
Minnesota State*, 65
Southern Indiana, 63
Toccoa Falls, 63

Sea Aggies
Texas A&M-Galveston, 71, 151

Sea Beggars
Providence Christian College, 42, 71

Sea Devils
Cape Fear CC, 71

Sea Gulls
Salisbury University, 56, 71

Sea Lions
UC Irvine, 12, 71

Seahawks, 67, 71

SeaWolves
Southern Maine CC, 71

Seawolves, 71
    Alaska-Anchorage, 88

Seceders
    Erskine College, 161

Seminoles
    Florida State, 72, 103-105

Setters
    Pace University, 151

Sharks, 70
    Landmark, 126

Shockers
    Wichita State, 52, 122

Silver Foxes
    Kent State, 153

Silver Helmets
    Colorado, 98

Silverswords
    Chaminade, 77, 109

Siwash
    Knox College, 113

Skipjacks
    Chesapeake College, 130

Skippers
    St. Clair County, 74

Skyhawks, 67

Skylights
    Montana State-Northern, 138

Snappers
    Spoon River, 55

Snortin' Swine
    Springfield A&M*, 65

Soaring Eagles
    Elmira College, 63

Sooners
    Oklahoma, 42, 106, 170-171

Sound
    Five Towns College, 42-43

Sourdoughs
    Alaska-Anchorage, 88

Spartans, 71
    Claremore Junior College, 156
    Michigan State, 133, 171

Spiders
    Richmond, 175

Spires
    Saint Mary, 151

Spirits
    Salem College, 151

Stags
    Fairfield, 100

Stallions
    Baldwin Agricultural, 64
    North American University, 64

Stampede
    Mesaland CC, 143

Staters
Michigan State, 133

Statesmen
Delta State, 23

Steels
Culinary Institute of America, 146

Steers
Texas College, 151

Stingrays
Coastal Pines Tech, 70

Stonewalls
Georgetown, 176

Storm, 80

Stormy Petrels
Oglethorpe University, 43

Stubby Christians
Springfield College, 131

Student Princes
Heidelberg University, 43-44

Sun Chiefs
Faulkner State, 86

Sun Devils
Arizona State, 88, 170

Sunbirds
Fresno Pacific, 55, 151

Sunblazers
Florida International, 103

Suncats
Central New Mexico, 64, 151

Sundodgers
Washington, 176

Sundogs
Great Plains College, 73

Surge
Cincinnati State, 151

Swedes
Bethany College, 121-122

Sycamores
Indiana State, 77

T

Tar Heels
North Carolina, 44, 106, 146-147

Tars
Rollins College, 44

Tartans
Carnegie Mellon, 68
Sinclair, 68

Tartars
Compton College, 93

Teachers
Central Missouri State, 137
Troy, 87

Techs
North Carolina State, 149

Tejanos
El Paso CC, 68

Terrapins
Maryland, 77, 127, 130

Terrible Swedes
Bethany College, 121-122

Terriers
Boston University, 131

Tetons
Williston State, 151

Texans
South Plains, 68
Tarleton State, 68, 97, 127

Thin Red Line
Alabama, 18

Thorobredettes
Kentucky State, 63

Thorobreds
Kentucky State, 63

Thoroughbreds
Murray State, 123
Skidmore, 63

Threshers
Bethel, 52

Thunder, 80

Thunderbirds
Mesa CC, 89
Rogers State, 156

Thunderducks
Dallas-Richland, 151

Thunderhawks
Miami University-Middletown, 67

Thundering Chickens
West Virginia Northern, 52, 176

Thundering Herd
Marshall, 177

Tigers, 5, 59, 64, 78-79
Auburn, 78, 85-86, 107, 171
Clemson, 25, 78, 107, 162
Edward Waters, 101
Florida A&M, 101
Grambling State, 170
Hampden-Sydney, 127
Howard College, 84
Jackson State, 97, 106, 171
LSU, 78, 125, 171
Memphis, 97, 170-171
Missouri, 78, 96, 170
Princeton, 37, 78
Tennessee State, 96, 106, 126
Texas Southern, 97, 126
Trinity, 78, 127

Titans, 71

Tomcats
Thiel College, 64

Tommies
St. Thomas, 78

Toreros
San Diego, 151

Tornado
King University, 80

Toros Salvajes
Universidad Autónoma de Chapingo, 74

Tortugas
Florida Keys, 127

Toucans
Universidad de Quintana Roo, 74

Tracers
Ohio-Zanesville, 151

Trailblazers
North Greenville, 161

Trappers
Northwest College, 74

Tree Frogs
North Seattle College, 53

Tree Planters
Nebraska, 139

Trekkers
McDowell Tech, 151

Tribunes
Monroe CC, 151

Triceratops
Cuyohoga CC, 23

Tritons
Missouri-St. Louis, 138

Trojans, 5, 71, 80
Coastal Carolina, 16
Southern California, 80, 93, 96
Taylor, 117-118
Troy, 87

Trolls
Trinity Christian, 71

Twins
Columbia-Greene, 151

U

Uhlan Chargers
University of Alabama in Huntsville, 85

Urban Knights
Academy of Art University, 50

Utes
Utah, 72, 107, 170-172

V

Valiants
Manhattanville University, 45

Valkyries
Converse, 72

Valor
Evangel University, 59

Vandals
Idaho, 109

V-Hawks
Viterbo University, 67

Vikings, 79
   Cleveland State, 127
   Ricks College, 110

Villains
   Manhattanville University, 45

Vixens
   Sweet Briar College, 23

Vols
   Logan College, 151

Volunteers, 5
   Tennessee, 45-47, 97, 164
   UHSP, 22

Voyageurs
   Minnesota North College – Rainy River, 135

Vulcans
   Hawaii-Hilo, 71
   PennWest California, 71

W

Wahoos
   Virginia, 173-174

War Hawks
   McMurray University, 67

Warhawks, 67

Warriors, 59, 60, 79
   Arkansas State, 90
   Gaston College, 147

Wasps
   Emory & Henry, 46-47

Wave
   Kingsborough CC, 151

Weberites
   Weber State, 172

Webfoots
   Oregon, 20-21, 156

Wesmen
   Winnipeg, 73

Westerners
   Western Texas, 78

Wheat Shockers
   Fairmont College, 122

Whitecaps
   Galveston College, 151

Whitetoppers
   Emory & Henry, 46-47

Wild Cats
   CC of Alleghany County, 53

WildCats
   Randolph, 151

Wildcats, 64, 79, 81
   Arizona, 81, 106, 170
   Bethune-Cookman, 81
   Cal State Chico, 81
   Kansas State, 61, 171
   Kentucky, 56, 81
   Northwestern, 81, 171
   Villanova, 81
   Weber State, 172

Wolf Pack
Nevada-Reno, 140

Wolfpack
North Carolina State, 97, 149

Wolverines, 6
Essex County College, 82
Grove City College, 82
Michigan, 82, 107, 171
Morris Brown College, 82
San Bernardino Valley, 82
Sierra College, 82
Utah Valley, 82

Wolves
Nevada-Reno, 140

Wombats
WGB-Sheboygan, 55

Wonder Boys
Arkansas Tech, 47

Wonder Girls
Arkansas Tech, 47

Wonderettes
Arkansas Tech, 47

Wood Ducks
Century College, 56

Wyverns
Quinsigamond CC, 71

X
X-Men
St. Francis Xavier, 73

X-Women
St. Francis Xavier, 73

Y
Yaks
Yakima Valley, 23, 55

Yellow Jackets
Black Hills State, 170
Georgia Tech, 105, 126

Yeomen
Oberlin, 154

Yeowomen
Oberlin, 154

Yetis
Cleveland CC, 71, 151

Z
Zippers, 179
Akron, 48

Zips
Akron, 48, 127

Other Considerations

Failed Nominees
- Antelopes, 165
- Aphids, 92
- Armadillos, 102
- Auctioneers, 149
- Baptist Bears, 84
- Boogercats, 177
- Bull Moose, 131
- Calumets, 149
- Cedars, 159
- Cheveliers, 48
- Coots, 102
- Cotton Pickers, 149
- Cows, 173
- Crackers, 104
- Cultivators, 149
- Cyclops, 125
- Daredevils, 125
- Electric Elk, 138
- Ferrets, 165
- Fighting Warriors, 104
- Flashers, 102
- Golden Blue Devils, 48
- Green Gobblers, 177
- Hamsters, 131
- Hillbillies, 48
- Hippopotamuses, 137
- Manatees, 102
- Mountain Boomers, 147
- Nodaks, 152
- North Staters, 149
- Pine-Rooters, 149
- Pinecones, 102
- Poets, 131
- Prather's Ground Hogs, 125
- River Rats, 118
- Rocks, 92
- Rubbernecks, 48
- Seagulls, 102
- Serpents, 125
- Skunks, 137
- Skyrockets, 153
- Sundogs, 152
- Tadpoles, 102
- Tarpons, 104
- Tip Toppers, 48
- Tom-Cats, 173
- Tomatoes, 142
- Vets, 134

About the Author

David Winder is a former sportswriter who is always on the lookout for good nicknames (teams and people). He patiently awaits the day the Fighting Giraffes become an official collegiate nickname. He also wrote a book about high school nicknames. There are no Fighting Giraffes there either.

Made in the USA
Coppell, TX
07 February 2026

70497577R00125